Also By Dr. Chris Miller:
I've Fallen And I Can Get Up! - The Ultimate Life Recovery Program (2011)

Get Up! COLLEGE

How to Successfully Navigate Your Freshman Year . . . and Beyond

DR. CHRIS MILLER

WESTBOW
PRESS®
A DIVISION OF THOMAS NELSON
& ZONDERVAN

WestBow Press books may be ordered through booksellers or by contacting:

WestBow Press
A Division of Thomas Nelson & Zondervan
1663 Liberty Drive
Bloomington, IN 47403
www.westbowpress.com
844-714-3454

ISBN: 978-1-4908-7968-0 (sc)
ISBN: 978-1-4908-7969-7 (e)

Library of Congress Control Number: 2015907290

Print information available on the last page.

WestBow Press rev. date: 08/06/2021

"If I could do it, so can you!"

TABLE OF CONTENTS

ACKNOWLEDGMENTS

I wish to thank Susan Balandran, M.A., for her helpful ideas during the initial stages of the *Get Up! College* book editing process. Also, I owe an enormous debt of gratitude to the many volunteer and focus group students who cheerfully donated time and energy so that the research necessary for this book could be conducted. Additionally, special thanks to the fine professional staff at WestBow Press for helping to make this book a reality. And last, but certainly not least, thank you Toby Spiegel, Psy.D., Patrick McKiernan, Ph.D., and Mark Morton, Ph.D., for your unwavering guidance and encouragement through the often painful rigors of research. And you're right, "it's worth it in the end!"

"It's not what preparing for college takes. It's what it takes if you don't."

FOREWORD

If the book, *Chicken Soup for the College Soul,* were likened to a meal appetizer, then *Get Up! College* would have to be described as "the main course."

Hello. This is Dr. Chris Miller. Welcome to *Get Up! College – How to Successfully Navigate Your Freshman Year . . . and Beyond.*

In my estimation, there will likely never be a shortage of books and campus guest speakers oozing with goose bump arousing stories, inspirational quotes and feel good chuckles to circulate the college market. After all, it's natural for nerve-frazzled students (and their parents I might add!) to demand such comforting material, especially upon embarking on the college journey. Because let's face it, who doesn't like to feel good? And what reasonable person, upon encountering significant stress, wouldn't seek comfort?

And while *Get Up! College* promises to provide a similar warm fuzzy experience, its ultimate objective is quite unique. In fact, the purpose of *Get Up! College* is to provide freshmen college students with the tools that research suggests will not only bring comfort, but will actually help more students succeed.

The truth of the matter is that many students desperately struggle to navigate a complex labyrinth of issues en route to successfully completing college. Developmental, financial, logistical, psychological, social, and substance abuse related issues represent just some of the many serious challenges that students are likely to face. And if left unchecked, any one of these is enough to sideline just about any student.

The fact is that forty-three percent of students who enroll in a college or university in America today will *not* graduate, even after 6 years. And what is especially startling about this statistic is that if a student is going to fail, more than half the time it will be in his or her freshman year!

However (and this is a *big* however!), the good news is that as a result of reading this book, your chances of successfully graduating from college are likely to climb exponentially—helping to ensure that you will *not* become an academic statistic. So stop stressing! (Ooh, I feel the goose bumps forming already!)

In fact, if you will do three simple things: 1) pay close attention to the most common reasons students fail, as outlined in Part One, 2) review my personal story, Part Two, and 3) learn about and apply the simple and easy to use strategies and techniques as outlined in Parts Two, Three and Four, then you will likely succeed.

Now for a caveat: for some students, research on virtually any subject may be likened to eating, well, shall we say, "Academic Brussels Sprouts!" So, while I keep the research that I'm about to share with you moving pretty quickly (oh, and "b-t-dubs," it's chalked full of some important info. too), nevertheless, by all means, skip ahead to Parts Two, Three and Four, and return to Part One to round out our time together, if you wish. (And don't worry, no one's going to call you a "lightweight" if you do :),

And most importantly, as we embark on this exciting journey together, if there is anything that I would like for you to bear in mind, it's this: *If I could graduate from college, then so can you!*

PART ONE

PART ONE

CHAPTER ONE

SCHOOLS STRETCHED THIN

When you get to the end of the rope, tie a knot and hang on.

-Franklin D. Roosevelt

Most would agree that trending on social media is a pretty cool thing. However, the kind of trending that I'm about to share with you, *isn't* so cool!

For example, according to educational researcher, Morisano (et al., 2010), of students who enroll in a four year college or university, 1 in 4 will never finish school. Were you aware of this? And only one-third of full-time college and university students in the United States will earn their degree within four years.

And on community college campuses where there is no traditional four year college experience, and where there are increased risk factors, for example, poverty (including parental stress related to money, unsafe neighborhoods, robust student work demands, lack of dorm life and peer support, being the first in the family to attend college, lack of role models and cultural understanding of higher education, and substance abuse issues), then according to researcher Navarro's 2012 study, student failure rates may be even higher.

And while approximately thirty-five percent of students depart a university for academic reasons, nearly two out of three students depart voluntarily for nonacademic reasons, such as anxiety, depression, adjustment problems, uncertain goals, shaky commitment, inadequate finances, lack of student involvement, and poor fit to the institution—this according to distinguished educational scholar, Vincent Tinto (1975, 2001, 2006-2007).

In fact, mental illness is the leading cause for withdrawal from an institution. And this all makes perfect sense, because college age students are at a prime age to develop psychological problems due in large part to dramatic changes naturally occurring within both body and brain.

As Dr. Frances Jensen reveals in her fascinating new book, *The Teenage Brain* (2015), a stressed eighteen to twenty-something year old is most likely to develop anxiety, depression, bipolar or schizophrenia. And this is *not* coincidental, because in order to manifest these symptoms, you need your prefrontal and frontal lobes, and these are not even connected until you enter college age.

Just imagine a parents shock to learn that their well-adjusted and otherwise perfectly normal son or daughter has just been diagnosed with depression! Or worse, that he or she has engaged in dangerous, self-injurious or other form of violent behavior, and are now suddenly forced to withdraw from school!

Now, combine such neurological shifts with a good dose of academic, social or financial stress, and then for good measure, throw in trending drug and alcohol abuse (not at all uncommon on college campuses—*you think?!*)—and voila!—a near perfect breeding ground for the development of clinically significant symptoms is spawned.

In fact, among students, parents, academics, mental health professionals and social scientists, there is now mounting concern regarding the growing mental health and life management needs of college students. And such concern is compounded by the fact that there are presently more needs than available resources.

Yes indeed, this "empty tap" on student mental health resources was forcefully brought to light by Gallagher's 2012 survey of colleges and universities representing 293 schools & 2.7 million students. According to this robust national study, the average ratio of counselors to students is a staggering 1 counselor to 1,600 students.

Now, to magnify how woefully ineffective this paucity of mental health resources has become, consider a 2010 survey of students by the American College Health Association. This study revealed that 45.6% of students reported feeling that things were hopeless, and 30.7% reported an episode of serious depression with difficulty functioning within the past 12 months.

And significantly, eighty-seven percent of college counseling center directors reported a steady increase in the numbers of students, 24%, arriving on campus who are *already* on psychotropic medication—a number growing significantly from 9% in 1994 (Gallagher, 2012).

And finally, 92% of college and university counseling center directors reported that the number of students seeking help at their center has increased over the past 5 years alone (Gallagher, 2012).

Some people interpret such data to mean that mental health needs assessment techniques have improved and are now more readily available to students, and that is all that is really occurring here. Others argue that today's student arrives on campus with considerably less intrapersonal, that is, "self," and interpersonal, that is, "social," resources necessary to cope with the day-to-day stressors of college life.

Either way, the development of mental resilience across the student population appears to be a worthwhile area of focus for students, concerned parents, college administrators and mental health professionals serious about academic success. And so you might wonder what is presently being done to reverse such unfavorable trends?

Well presently, in order to address the growing needs of students with psychological problems, Gallagher's study

(2012) concluded that 73% of college and university counseling center directors reported that noncritical clients are seen less frequently; 66% report that staff increase caseloads at busy times and reduce other involvements; 50% report making use of more external referrals; 46% report putting more focus on brief therapy models; 42% report moving to a "no automatic weekly appointments—students are seen as schedule permits" model; and 41% reported hiring new counseling staff or hiring part-time staff during busy times. And all of this at a time when campus budget cuts and skyrocketing tuition costs converge to present a very real and growing national crisis.

Now, more specifically with regards to how college counseling staff spend their time, the average staff counselor reportedly spent 24 hours per week providing one-to-one counseling; 6 hours in other direct services to students, for example, group workshops and presentations; and 10 hours in other activities, for instance, clinical notes, staff meetings, supervision, contact with faculty, parents and others.

This means that (on average) only approximately 16% of a counselor's time can possibly be devoted to direct student prevention and student resiliency related services. A majority of the time appears to be spent addressing student needs one-to-one, and significantly, *after* clinical symptoms have already formed.

This model barely meets the needs of the otherwise well-functioning student who develops acute clinical symptoms.

Therefore, it can hardly be relied upon to adequately address the needs of students suffering with significant, what might be termed, "hard," developmental deficits (for example, social developmental deficits), which require more, not less, intervention. And herein lies the problem that our nation's college campuses are faced with, especially since resources to fund college counseling programs are becoming increasingly difficult to obtain.

And really, this issue of mental health related challenges outpacing available resources is not just a college problem, but a national one. In fact, it's a problem that strikes at the very heart of the *methods* by which mental health services are presently delivered across our culture more broadly.

Because, as we just reviewed, the most common method of mental health delivery is one-to-one care. And that is why (especially for college students) a primary assumption of this book is that one-to-one counselor to student mental health delivery will no longer suffice.

Now for another important caveat: I am an advocate of one-to-one counseling and psychotherapy. There will always be a need for individual care. In fact, I have provided such services myself for many years, and still do.

However, while it remains true that college counseling centers are needed now more than ever before, they cannot possibly meet student needs when serving as a primary and standalone approach to addressing mental health challenges, as the one-to-one approach has traditionally been relied upon to do. And that is why a suggested paradigm shift in the way that mental health services are offered to students is a key component of this book.

I believe that in order to truly impact the mental health challenges so often responsible for spiking failure rates of college students, mental health professionals must increasingly think outside of the four walls of the traditional counseling office.

After all, how much can be done to stem the rising tide of mental health challenges on our nation's campuses when services are focused merely one student at a time? Instead, thinking must shift toward large scale mental health education and mental illness prevention and intervention programs.

And another consideration is that of thinking less about deficits- or illness- or weakness-based approaches to mental health delivery. Instead, the focus ought to be on helping students access their strengths—what might aptly be termed a "solution-oriented" approach. And of course, this paradigm shift represents another key component of the *Get Up! College* philosophy of student success.

In Part Four, where we discuss the *Get Up! College* boot camp and class, just how this positive shift occurs in the lives of students will be further explained. And it's really quite simple. In fact, students can use many of the exercises in the comfort of home or in the convenience of a dorm room.

And so now the following question will likely begin to emerge: Why is all of this information important to me as a student?

Well, I'm glad you asked!

It's important for three reasons: 1) it alerts you to the realities of what tens of thousands of other students, just like you, will encounter in the coming school year, 2) it helps remove the mystery and stigma often associated with anxiety, depression and other psychological challenges, and 3) it will likely help you value and implement this book's strategies and techniques so that *you* won't become another statistic! And that's precisely why in the chapters to follow, we'll review what research has to say about what students need most.

CHAPTER TWO

STUDENTS NEED SOCIAL SUPPORT

Learning would be exceedingly laborious, not to mention hazardous, if people had to rely singularly on the effects of their own actions to inform them what to do.

-Albert Bandura

According to pioneering educator, psychologist, and social scientist, Albert Bandura (1986), Most human behavior is learned observationally through modeling: by observing others one forms an idea of how new behaviors are performed. And on later occasions this coded information serves as a guide for action.

According to researcher, Peele (1992), social learning theory as proposed by Albert Bandura has become perhaps the most influential theory of learning and development. His theory is rooted in many basic concepts of traditional learning theory and has had a substantial effect on education.

Bandura believed that direct reinforcement (a concept popularized within the schools of behavioral theory) could not account for all types of learning. Therefore, his theory added both social *and* cognitive elements.

According to Peele (1992), Bandura argued that people learn from other people. And so there are three core elements of Bandura's teaching model: 1) observation via a live model, 2) a verbal model, and 3) a symbolic model made up of fictional characters in the form of books, film and television. He taught that people can learn through observation from these and other mediums.

Additionally, he believed that mental states are important in learning. Perhaps that is why Albert Bandura and others often referred to his social learning theory as "cognitive learning theory."

The cognitive elements of Bandura's theory promote that learning takes place during the modeling process. Bandura believed that instruments and forces in the form of observational stimuli, cognition and people (within the context of environment) are the primary drivers of learning and human development.

According to Bandura (1986), learning does not necessarily lead to changes in behavior. Certain requirements and steps must be followed for learning to occur. And some of these steps involve both learner and model (such as "reproduction"), where coach, mentor, peer group and classroom models are employed.

He also promoted cognition in the form of properly focusing ones thoughts, and motivation in the form of goals (elements that are well represented by empirical research as effective means of learning and human change).

Bandura's well-established views help us better understand ways in which the educational constructs of learning and human development play a potentially crucial role in decreasing student stress, increasing student resilience and promoting first year college student success.

That is why in this chapter we will examine two important social models, 1) coach/mentor and 2) peer models, both of which research indicates are especially effective for helping college students succeed.

Out of Bandura's work comes role modeling and life coach mentoring, both significant agents of human change. In fact, some researchers believe that modeling provides the most effective means of skill development and behavioral change that is presently available. However, unfortunately, coach/mentoring is an all too often lost art in the U.S. today.

And yet, Gray's (et al., 2014) study points out that research provides empirical evidence that life coaching programs can facilitate goal attainment, improve mental health and enhance ones quality of life.

And with regards to peer support, student peers can play a valuable role in college student success. In 2010, Evans and fellow researchers pointed out that most student development theories attribute great significance to the process of maturation with respect to social relationship skill building resulting from intensive interaction with peers within the context of a growth-oriented group and mentoring relationship.

In fact, the powerful impact of peers in human development has been widely documented for decades, extending at least as far back as Clark & Trow, 1966, and Feldman & Newcomb, 1969, who first researched the powerful role of peer influence on college culture. Since that time, according to Whiteman's (et al., 2013) study, research in support of peer support has increased significantly.

In 2001, researchers Ender and Kay (sounds a bit like a cosmetics line, but it's not) conducted a meta-analysis of research on peer leadership and identified many important trends in the movement toward an increasing use of peer mentors in college and university education programs. Among the primary reasons cited by Ender and Kay is the finding that peer mentor, coach and educator models, when instituted well, work particularly well toward helping students succeed.

And in 2010, Evans and fellow researchers summarized an entire body of research on this subject to conclude that the dynamic of peer mentor support has had a positive effect upon virtually every aspect of freshman student life (not the least of which, academic progress and success).

Such a positive dynamic is especially helpful for students residing in off-campus housing, aka, "commuter students."

Commuter student's make up an overwhelming majority of the college student population, especially among community colleges. And what we understand thus far is that commuter students represent a particularly diverse mix of students. So their need for support is significant.

Hintz' 2011 study cites numerous reasons why commuter students are particularly at risk of dropping out of school, and why it is that for such students peer leaders are particularly helpful.

The primary reasons he suggests from his research, as well as via a meta-analysis of the subject, include the following: commuter students report feeling disconnected and marginalized from the life of the campus—producing less self-identification as a college student who "belongs," heart and soul, to a particular institution; focus on getting basic needs met, such as food, housing and transportation can distract students from making academic progress; and living off-campus can lead to academic and social isolation, typically providing less accountability and peer support.

As colleges and universities grapple to meet the many complex needs of today's diverse college student body, it is likely that this growing trend of utilizing peer, coach, mentor, educator and leadership support (particularly upon yielding such positive benefit) will continue to grow.

However, it's important to remember that successful peer programs do not merely emerge by happenstance, but instead must be thoughtfully and strategically established. Because just as great good can come from peer mentoring, so can great harm, to both the mentored and the mentor him- or herself.

That is why, according to leading researchers, peer leadership programs are typically most effective when they are established and/or monitored by a trained professional.

In conclusion of this chapter, it's important to note that this research is vitally important, because it helps us see the important role that social support plays in the lives of students. We will return to this subject a bit further along in our time together. "I pinky swear!"

STUDENTS NEED COGNITIVE RESILIENCE

The mind is its own place, and in itself can make a Heaven or Hell.

-John Milton, Paradise Lost

Welcome to Chapter Three research on the subject of students' need of cognitive resilience. Upon hearing the word, *cognitive*, some of you are likely asking, "Whaaat?" Well, when we talk about cognition, we're merely talking about *thoughts*. Cognition relates to our thoughts and perceptions—essentially, the way in which we interpret life events.

And what about cognitive psychology? Well, it's like Electronic Dance Music (EDM), but with zero after effects!

In fact, research from both meta-analytic reviews (a fancy way of saying, "a broad review of research literature on the subject"), as well as independent studies, support the effectiveness of cognitive-based approaches to treatment. And significantly, cognitive therapy has been shown to assist in reducing acute distress often associated with a broad range of clinical symptoms.

Further research exists to support the notion that cognitive forms of intervention appear to have an enduring effect, preventing the return of symptoms post-successful treatment. This all means that cognitive interventions in the lives of students tend to "stick" well.

Cognitive interventions can redirect the flow of brain electro chemicals, supplying an immediate mood lifter. We'll discuss how this occurs in Part Three—so hang in there!

According to research, cognitive therapy is also found to be efficacious in the acute treatment of moderately and severally depressed outpatients, while positive thoughts appear to serve as a stress mediator. And finally, according to research conducted by Strunk (et al., 2010), the efficacy of cognitive therapy (CT) for depression is well-established. While Wong's 2010 study lends increasing support for the role of cognitive interventions in the lives of students relative to balanced states of mind (BSOM) in psychopathology and psychological wellbeing.

Wong reported that there are unique themes of semantic content in self-reported automatic negative thoughts, particularly with regard to depression and anxiety. This study investigated the balanced states of mind model and its cognitive content specificity for depression, anxiety, anger, stress, life satisfaction and happiness based on negative and positive automatic thoughts. Three hundred and ninety-eight college students from Singapore participated in the study.

This study found that positive automatic thoughts are positively correlated with happiness and life satisfaction, and negatively correlated with stress, anxiety, depression and anger—among the most common symptoms reported among college students, and the symptoms most often attributed to student crisis-related reasons for dropping out of school (Eisenberg et al., 2009). And finally, positive thoughts are also identified as a buffer against campus violence.

In contrast, negative automatic thoughts were positively correlated with violence, stress, anxiety, depression and anger, and negatively correlated with life satisfaction and happiness.

This study concluded that coping with stress and psychological wellbeing is a function of the BSOM ratio of positive thoughts to the sum of positive and negative thoughts. And interestingly, the results further suggest that the more moderately positive thoughts one has, the better mental health outcomes can be expected. After all, we don't want to become overly manic, do we? (We'll reserve that for when we cheer-on our favorite school team!)

This study suggests that real world thinking is bound to bring some negative and challenging thoughts, but that mental health is best achieved when these are balanced and counteracted by positive thoughts. In the case of many students, the ratio is more negative thoughts to positive thoughts, and this is what we are trying to counteract in helping students improve cognitive resilience.

Additional examples of cognitive interventions include a 2011 study by Hughes and fellow researchers revealing the effectiveness of students learning to actively challenge negative thoughts by the use of a cognitive technique known as "reframing." After training a set of students about how to reframe circumstances and events in their lives, stress levels were compared with students receiving only cliché feedback and lecture about the topic, as opposed to actively applying the exercise to the circumstance or situation.

Outcomes revealed that students who applied the cognitive reframing exercises to their lives experienced significantly less stress related to life incidence than those from the control group. Additionally, students involved in the reframing activity group reported feeling good about the exercise and said they enjoyed it.

Additional research worth noting comes from Morin (2005) and Seaward (2006) who identified the importance of reframing negative self-talk as stress and mood management techniques potentially useful to students experiencing enormous pressure while embarking on the college experience for the first time.

These studies suggest potentially positive implications for exercises such as Positive Personal and Peer Affirmations (PPPA), Challenging Distorted Beliefs (CDB) and Automatic

Negative Thought Stopping (ANTS—be careful, because they can really eat your lunch if you let 'em!).

These three exercises are specific to cognitive therapy and cognitive psycho-education, and thus, are central to this *Get Up! College* success program. These will be alluded to in my personal story, Part Two, and then prescribed, explained and practiced by you, the student, when we arrive at Parts Three and Four.

Additionally, cognitive interventions are among the most user-friendly of clinical interventions when compared with some other treatment modalities (psychoanalysis for example). Some treatment modalities take years and potentially hundreds of hours of psychotherapy (to the tune of thousands of dollars!) in order to produce a net effect.

And what's really cool is that cognitive exercises can be used both within individual *and* group environments. Therefore, they are particularly well-suited for the college classroom and campus social setting.

And finally, recent studies in mindfulness interventions among younger generations have highlighted the efficacy of promoting wellbeing (a positive, forward looking, preventive and solution focused approach), as opposed to merely treating symptoms. Such studies are rich in samples examining younger subjects, yielding findings that are particularly important for professionals working with today's college student body.

According to many researchers, the transition from high school to college represents a distinct developmental period wherein a variety of psychosocial stressors represent. And since there is nothing that can be done, nor should there be, to remove reality, such stressors often lead to substance abuse among college populations.

Fromm further found that students who received a cognitively applied substance abuse intervention reported lower quantity and frequency of drinking when compared with no intervention. And since according to Fromm, a national sample of seventy-seven thousand first year U.S. college students showed that risky drinking increased within the first few weeks of college (and continued from there), early interventions in the form of preventive education (for which cognitive interventions are also uniquely positioned) provides tremendous value.

In fact, numerous researchers, such as Hunt (et al., 2014), Hartley (2011), and others argue that cognitive interventions promote *efficient mental health delivery systems* (allowing far more students to be screened and helped), *because* they are particularly suited for the "hustle & bustle" lifestyle of today's college student.

And with additional reference to efficiency, further research from Fromm indicates that group interventions are deemed just as effective as one-to-one interventions for helping to lower incidence of college student alcohol abuse.

This may be interpreted as further supporting broader (working with multiple students as opposed to merely focusing on one individual student at a time) prevention-based delivery systems.

And further regarding cognitive interventions and efficiency of application, meta-analysis of empirical research suggests that cognitive-oriented interventions are effective for a wide range of disorders.

For instance, after extensive review of twenty-eight peer reviewed research articles factoring in carefully controlled conditions covering twenty-six different studies comparing a cognitive approach to other psychotherapies, the superiority of cognitive approaches was apparent among patients suffering from anxiety and depression. (And remember, anxiety and depression are among the chief reasons, according to Eisenberg—et al., 2009—as identified in a robust University of Michigan study, for why students drop out of school!)

And by the way (or, for those who prefer, "b t dubs" :), the University of Michigan has something of real value to say on this subject. Bolstered by a pioneering "Cadillac" mental health outreach and mental health education and wrap-around program for its students, the University of Michigan boasts the lowest failure rate of any university in the nation—only 5%!

And finally, Tolin's 2010 study suggests that cognitive approaches should be considered a front of line psychosocial treatment of choice, particularly among students suffering with anxiety and depression. While 2012 research by Witthoft and fellow researchers shows a positive correlation between somatic symptoms and distress related to unresolved negative experiences and memories. These studies further fortify the notion that cognitive exercises may be particularly helpful in ameliorating a broad range of stressors and symptoms experienced by many of today's college students.

CHAPTER FOUR

POSITIVE PSYCHOLOGY

"If you wish to become confident and cover an entire ocean of personal deficiencies, then master a skill. Become great at something!"

-The Author

For the positive psychologist, foundational questions are *What is?* and *What could be?* And much like the *Get Up! College* philosophy of student success, the focus is not so much on revisiting the past or seeking in-depth understanding of the nature of mankind. Instead, it's that of helping students identify and utilize their strengths.

According to pioneering positive psychologist, Martin Seligman, the positive psychologist views this strengths-based approach as providing a natural buffer against weakness. And researcher, Linley et al., in a 2010 study, asserted that "the science of positive psychology is the study of psychological strengths relative to positive emotions."

The insight for this new way of viewing the human experience came differently for each of the founding pioneers of positive psychology. For Seligman, it was an encounter with his then five year old daughter that opened his eyes to the need for a change in treatment focus. However, Seligman's fellow researcher, Csikszentmihalyi, realized the need for a positive psychology in Europe during World War II. As a child, he witnessed those who endured circumstances of the war with strength, despite their relatively humble social, material or educational means.

He observed that many of those who formerly were known as successful and self-confident (possessing good jobs, wealth, education and social prowess) became helpless and dispirited once stripped of these social supports. And there were few who kept their integrity and purpose despite the surrounding difficulty.

This led Csikszentmihalyi to wonder what sources of strength these people were drawing on. In fact, such questioning nourished the soil from which the discipline of positive psychology eventually emerged.

Positive psychology is not merely a study of the ravages of mental illness, but more so a study of human strength and virtue—hence the formulation of the name of this approach to helping people. And treatment is not merely about fixing what is broken, but of nurturing what is best.

Due to this focus, prevention is fundamental to positive psychology. And positive psychologists maintain that the "disease" and "deficiencies" focused or "magical doctor to sick patient" model does not move the field of mental health closer to prevention. In fact, they contend that it moves it further away. And it appears that they are right.

Perhaps that is why, despite a plethora of mental health professionals existing within the United States today (many of whom rely on the medical or disease model of intervention), there remains considerable dysfunction and pathology among the U.S. population.

Such a reality (as alluded to earlier) points to the need for a reexamination of traditional approaches to intervention. It also highlights the need for a more hopeful, positive and preventive approach—particularly for incoming college freshman whose experience may have more parallels to a world war than many people may realize!

Seligman and Csikszentmihalyi maintain that "large strides have come from a perspective focused on systematically building competency, not on correcting weakness," and that "Prevention researchers have discovered that there are human strengths that act as buffers against mental illness." Among these are courage, future mindedness, optimism, interpersonal skill, faith, work ethic, hope, honesty and perseverance.

They further contend that much of the discussion of the twenty-first century will be to create a science of human strength, whose mission will be to understand and foster such strengths in the lives of young people, thus denoting an entire transformation of culture.

In a 2009 study, Seligman and fellow researchers defined positive education as education for both traditional skills and for happiness, and argued that schools *can* and *should* teach positive values—a suggestion that seems to run contrary to prevailing trends for many U.S. colleges and universities today.

Following an intensive literature meta-analysis on the subject, Seligman and Csikszentmihalyi maintain that large strides have *already* come from a perspective focused on systematically building competency, as opposed to merely correcting weakness.

And significant studies through the Seligman-led University of Pennsylvania Resiliency Program, or PRP, and Strath Haven Positive Psychology Curriculum, are pointed to as evidence for such conclusions.

PRP is one of the most widely researched programs designed to prevent depression in young people ages 8-15. In fact, during the past 20 years, 17 studies have evaluated PRP in comparison to randomized controlled designs with over 2,000 children and adolescents between the ages of 8 and 15, according to Horowitz & Garber's 2006 research analysis.

Additionally, a fairly recent meta-analysis of research on depression prevention programs for young people found thirty studies in total. And a primary thrust of several studies specifically comparing PRP interventions with control groups showed superior benefits for PRP in reducing and preventing depression and anxiety and hopelessness.

The PRP program targets strengths, the promotion of resilience, the development of positive emotion and the student's sense of meaning and purpose.

In PRP classes, discussions of character strengths, promotion and utilization of natural skills, social skill development, expression of positive emotions and a special component focused on challenging distorted beliefs while maintaining a 3 to 1 positive to negative cognitive thought ratio are also emphasized.

And recent breakthroughs in neuroscience research and brain plasticity studies further support the role of the brain and an individuals' thoughts with respect to mental health, according to researchers Boyle and Wong (as expressed in each of their 2010 studies).

Perhaps that is why, increasingly, researchers are concluding that it seems fitting to have focused attention on cognitive interventions as a means of more efficiently addressing mental health issues, particularly among the college population.

In fact, Wong's 2010 study in particular cites recent breakthroughs in neuroscience research that has shed light on the curative and preventive effects of various cognitive exercises. And my own 2014 meta-analysis suggests that exercises which can be easily taught within a student classroom setting, and then further implemented as practice at home, appear to be particularly useful.

And MRI research provides compelling evidence to suggest that cognitive-based interventions successfully treat anxiety and produce brain changes that have a directly meditative role on brain function and symptom reduction.

And with further reference to brain plasticity ("plasticity" as used here simply refers to the brains ability to change and adapt), students may well benefit by understanding the ways in which neuroscience (and brain plasticity studies in particular) promote encouraging perspectives with regard to what is humanly possible.

Formerly, the prevailing view in the scientific community was that the brain remained fixed throughout a person's life. However, it is now becoming evident that human beings have the capacity to alter their own brains, at least to some degree.

In a 2010 study, Cacioppo and fellow researchers provided evidence that events at one level of an organism, that is, molecules, cells, organs and individual behavior, can profoundly affect events at other levels. And researchers Reik, Dean & Walter (2001) and Suomi (1999) have all discovered evidence of social influence with regard to both the constitution of genes, and their expressive function.

The implication here is that environmental triggers, such as stress, emotion, focused social support, cognitive intervention, and goal-oriented motivation can radically alter our genes through reprogramming—so that we can in fact influence our genetic material. And the ability to influence one's own genetic structure can potentially minimize the daunting belief that some students are born with limitations that cannot be overcome.

This is wildly significant! I think of those students who may be the first in their family to attend college or university. This information may be particularly meaningful to such students in light of research suggesting that belief in one's ability to persevere in the face of adversity (despite heredity) may act as a stress and mood moderator. And this is precisely the kind of information that we want to be sure and highlight in our work with today's diverse student population.

CHAPTER FIVE

STUDENTS NEED GOALS

Obstacles are those frightful things you see when you take your eyes off your goals.

-Henry Ford

According to Perry (1991) and Stupniski (et al., 2007), many of the changes a student goes through in transitioning from high school to college can adversely influence student perceptions of control. And issues of students' sense of control is arguably a more powerful predictor of GPA than self-esteem.

And according to Perry (1991) and fellow researchers, such changes increase student emphasis on success, competition, pressure to excel, dissolution with steep learning curves, as well as numerous other stressful challenges. As a result, significant change may potentially contribute to decreased academic performance and increased dropout rates, as demonstrated in several studies of college classrooms.

The importance of Morisano and fellow researchers' 2010 study (as cited earlier) lies in the suggestion that many of these stressors are significantly ameliorated in the presence of immersion into a goals program. Research related to goals training primarily exists within the field of industrial-organizational ("I-O") psychology literature. However, a relatively smaller but substantial body of literature exists with regards to goal setting in academic contexts as well.

Morisano and fellow researchers suggest that student grades, retention rates, ability to complete more courses per semester, as well as persistence and personal levels of student motivation, increase when students are immersed in goal setting as a part of their academic preparation.

Goal setting theory emerged within the field of industrial-organizational psychology over the course of the past thirty-five years. In fact, according to Latham & Locke's 2007 research, more than four hundred correlation and experimental studies provide evidence for the validity of the goal setting approach.

Additionally, goals-orientation has arisen as a primary component of the science of positive psychology, which, according to Linley's 2008 study, tends to focus on psychological strengths and positive emotions that are energizing and which lead to maximum effectiveness.

In fact, within coaching psychology literature, focusing on strengths is demonstrated to be associated with both subjective and psychological wellbeing. According to this framework, successful achievement involves positive feedback loops between self-efficacy and goal commitment.

The net effect of setting goals has been extensively researched, including effective delivery methods with regard to best practice for the application of goals. And that is why significant support exists for the notion that students are better served when goal setting exercises are strategically and skillfully crafted by a coach or mentor. In fact, according to 2012 research conducted by Shook & Keup (not to be confused with "chicken coop!"), the potential benefits of employing on-campus programs wherein a structured coach-led component can be utilized is highly recommended.

In conclusion, research related to college and university student success consists of a labyrinth of elements. The variety of such elements is seemingly as complex as the lives of students themselves. However, upon close inspection, distinct trends emerge. And it is these trends that *Get Up! College* seeks to address.

PART TWO

PART TWO

THE MESSAGE

(A message by Dr. Miller for incoming college students, entitled, *If I could do it, so can you!*)

Message Provided Via CD <u>or</u> Journal

Man often becomes what he believes himself to be. If I keep on saying to myself that I cannot do a certain thing, it is possible that I may end by really becoming incapable of doing it. On the contrary, if I have the belief that I can do it, I shall surely acquire the capacity to do it even if I may not have it at the beginning.

-Mahatma Gandhi

PART THREE

PART THREE

CHAPTER SIX

COGNITIVE HOT SPOTS

All that we are is the result of what we have thought.

-Buddha

In the cellular world, "hot spots" indicate significant communication activity. This is typically considered a positive thing. After all, who likes dropped calls?

However, for purposes of this chapter, we will use the term "cognitive hot spots" to denote something negative, symbolizing inaccurate, negative, toxic, anxious or depressed thoughts (obviously *not* a good thing). And remember (from an earlier section), "cognition" refers to the psychological structures, processes and thoughts that shape our perspectives about, and reactions to, life events.

The subject of cognitive hot spots is especially important to students (and really, to everyone!), because inaccurate, negative, "toxic" or depressed thoughts can get students into serious trouble. In fact (as mentioned already), leading contributors to student failure are anxiety and depression, two of the more common cognitive hot spots. (Anxiety and depression are related. Just think of them as nasty, incestuous "kissing cousins," a disturbing image that you'll likely not forget!)

Now, before we apply the exercises so helpful to overcoming cognitive hot spots, I thought it would be helpful to discuss some of the more common ones. It will be interesting to see how many of the following cognitive hot spots you can identify with.

The first cognitive hot spot that students often suffer is, "lack of clarity." In the scriptures (Luke's gospel, Chapter 14 and verses 28-32), Jesus asks:

"For which one of you, when he wants to build a tower, does not first sit down and calculate the cost, to see if he has enough to complete it? Otherwise, when he has laid a foundation and is not able to finish, all who observe it begin to ridicule him, saying, 'This man began to build and was not able to finish.' Or what king, when he sets out to meet another king in battle, will not first sit down and take counsel whether he is strong enough with ten thousand men to encounter the one coming against him with twenty thousand? Or else, while the other is still far away, he sends a delegation and asks terms of peace."

Oftentimes, we fail because we venture forth without clarity. Therefore, I often ask my students, *What is it that you truly want for your life?* And almost always the answer is the same, "happiness."

As stated earlier, happiness is certainly a very positive emotion to desire. After all, who doesn't want to be happy?

However, the problem with such a vague response is that it lacks specificity, and therefore, clarity. It is only as I probe deeper that I learn more definitively what "happiness" represents to an individual at any given point in time.

As a result, I am often amazed at how many students drift through school without a clear and specific plan of action. Having only a vague idea of what they truly want out of their studies (and from life in general), and moving forward in a nonchalant and haphazard manner, they experience very little extraordinary results, and typically quite a few disastrous ones! They then become discouraged and quit.

In fact, I have sometimes wondered if the unhappiness, emptiness and boredom that some students are prone to experience results from failing to engage a bigger vision for their academic studies, their careers, and for their lives.

"The purpose of life is to discover your gift. The work of life is to develop it. The meaning of life is to give your gift away."

-David Viscott

Therefore, it is absolutely essential that you invest time in understanding yourself, your goals and your deepest passion(s) for living. Because, only once you have invested the time to become absolutely clear about what you truly want are you ready to take significant action.

The reason for this is simply that anything worth accomplishing will be met with some degree of difficulty, and therefore, will naturally require proper planning and persistent effort. Otherwise, you might easily fall victim to defeat—as the examples of both the builder of the tower, and the king (as cited above) so richly illustrate.

The next common cognitive hot spot relates to "codependence." This is problematic for many students. And yet, it is impossible to be your best self when you settle for relationships that you *know* (deep inside) are sucking the life right out of you.

Most of us crave intimacy and the good feelings that come from being in a romantic relationship with someone for whom we have affection. This is normal. However, when we remain in an unhealthy or abusive relationship, especially one that puts our personal safety or that of our loved ones at risk, or runs contrary to our academic and life's goals, values and interests, then we greatly limit ourselves.

Bargaining through a codependent relationship often travels along one or more of these lines: "I can't live without him or her" or "He or she needs me" or "What if no one else wants me?" or "I just can't stand to be alone" or "I can't graduate without meeting my life's partner. If I am going to get married, it will only come to me while I am in college" or "What if I don't make it on my own?" or "He will be so angry and may try to hurt me."

For some of you the abuse suffered at the hands of an emotionally distant parent or other authority figure was the only time that you felt a connection to that person. The abuse was anything but easy to endure. It hurt. But it felt better than being ignored. When this figure in your life acted abusively, at least they were engaging you while the abuse was taking place.

In such cases, a semblance of intimacy is derived by being abused. This pattern is then perpetuated by selecting similar dynamics in future relationships, which becomes especially easy to do with the freedom and potential loneliness that can sometimes accompany going off to school.

Our baseline stress level, what we could call, "a normal degree of stress," is not set for life. Life experiences can, and do, reset our brain's "stress thermostat" at a higher level, so that we experience higher levels of stress reactivity if we have been exposed to particularly intense or repeated stressors within a short timeframe, or if we've been exposed to emotional trauma.

A student who remains in a particular "state," such as a stress state, for too long, potentially risks stabilizing that state within the nervous system. For instance, experiencing normal levels of conflict or stress in a relationship is not necessarily a problem. The problem develops when we fail to do anything about it—we allow the conflict and the stress state that goes with it to persist. The longer the state persists, the more reinforced and familiar it becomes to the nervous system. It becomes comfortable—home. It should then come as little surprise when we unwittingly seek that state out of familiarity or comfort.

This dynamic of homeostasis (which means, "home state"), more loosely referred to as, "comfort level," manifests as an attraction to, or increased comfort with, stressful, chaotic or emotion-laden relationship experiences. The home state is that state to which we have become accustomed. Therefore, we choose it time and again, oftentimes without realizing why.

(IMPORTANT SIDE NOTE: *And truthfully, many first generation freshmen college students feel out of their comfort zone. They ask themselves, "Do I even belong here in college?" And the correct answer is, "Yes, you belong!" Just set your goals and ignore these new and oftentimes overwhelming feelings. In time your brain chemistry, i.e., homeostasis, will shift to embrace this new experience :),*

You can get out of an abusive or codependent cycle by first weighing the cost of remaining in the relationship (and by the way, seeing yourself as valuable is paramount here), then by working with a professional to obtain a greater degree of emotional health and strength. Also, forming a support network, generating a plan of action or escape, and capturing a desire to begin living with a higher purpose in mind are essential as well.

I have met many students who offer themselves at the altar of destructive relationships. They diminish their potential for growth, personal freedom and academic success, and instead merely plug along in a state of silent desperation. They later spend much of their lives thinking, "What if?" or "If only I had!" Welcome to the "What if" club!

Fear of the unknown, of leaving the familiar, forms a powerful shackle. Manipulated by voices that say, "you can't" or "I can't" can be overcome only by taking that first step. Then, as if alive for the very first time, you discover that a whole new world is there for the taking, and that you *can* move forward toward something much better. If this describes you, then my sincere hope is that you will tap into the courage that oftentimes lies dormant within you to break free and begin *really* living!

The third major cognitive hot spot for students relates to dysthymia, major depression, and anxiety.

On any given day, approximately twenty-five million Americans (roughly one in twelve people) feel down in the dumps and suffer some of the symptoms of depression. This is particularly true among freshman college students. The relatively carefree days of high school being gone, students suddenly find themselves under enormous stress.

Dysthymia is a milder, yet persistent and often overlooked form of depression. It can be hard to identify, because, while the symptoms are similar, dysthymia is not as severe as major depression. However, these less severe symptoms often last for a period of two years or longer. And dysthymia can be particularly difficult to identify among college students because stress, and its accompanying energy drain, can be chalked up as a normal part of the college experience.

Dysthymia robs students of their vitality and zest for life. A student will often become irritable. The crispness and clarity necessary for remaining academically focused, making good decisions, as well as personal confidence, are stripped. In this low grade depression, the color of life has imperceptibly melted away.

Major depression is different. It is often debilitating. It is cunning, in that, the student suffering with major depression is often the last to identify it as such. Some chief characteristics of major depression include: depressed mood, irritability, excessive guilt, fatigue or loss of energy, changes in sleep and/ or appetite, excessive crying for no apparent reason, suicidal ideas, and wherein there is significant anger or tendencies toward violence, even homicidal ideas focused on fellow students. Additionally, there is often poor decision making resulting from confusion, loss of interest in pleasurable things, and negative perceptions and thoughts. Ultimately, depression ranges from mild to moderate to severe.

"Hope alone is a powerful antidepressant," writes David Burns, M.D. And hope is what this book is ultimately all about!

General anxiety disorder, eating disorders, obsessive compulsive disorder (OCD), post-traumatic stress disorder (PTSD), panic attacks, phobias and other forms of anxiety emerge for a variety of reasons. And while the intent of this book is not to go in-depth into each of these, it may prove useful to keep in mind that they are physiologically and brain-based; they are environmentally triggered and/or nurtured; and they are treatable.

The information and exercises in this book should prove helpful toward managing depression and anxiety. Of course, any clinical disorder should be managed under the care of a mental health professional or physician.

Then we have "False Failure." This is a biggie for many students, particularly for those of you feeling the pressure that others have placed upon you.

> *Let the world know you as you are, not as you think you should be.*
>
> -Unknown Author

False failure is a psychosocially rooted false perception of failure that occurs when we, despite doing quite well, are bombarded with messages to the contrary. Some of us actually become frozen with fear. We believe we will never do, or be, good enough. But to admit such fear, we believe, would bring shame. So we suffer in silence.

In some cases, our lives become pre-scripted by those well intentioned (and sometimes not so well intentioned!) individuals, parents, extended family members and friends who endeavor to control how our life is supposed to be lived, even down to the very last detail. For example, the parent who pushes their son toward becoming a world class business mogul, when in reality, the son dislikes business. Instead, he prefers painting and photography.

This particular variety of pressure is most often found on Ivy League or otherwise long established and competitive college and university campuses. For students dealing with this sort of pressure, the exercises and principles found in this book will likely be a real breathe of fresh air.

Ralph Waldo Emerson once wrote, "To be yourself in a world that is constantly trying to make you into something else is the greatest accomplishment."

Unwittingly, we can fall into the trap of adopting other peoples' definition of success instead of our own. We assume an identity based on the expectations of others, and become so embroiled in what we *think* we are supposed to do, that we lose sight of our own definition of success and personal fulfillment.

In particularly persuasive or shame-based cultures and subcultures, "wandering from the chosen path" can be met with intense and stifling guilt—a dynamic that research indicates is most common among students representing Middle Eastern, Asian, and dogmatic religious populations.

We wake up one day and have to face the fact that we have not met the expectations of others, but cannot figure out why. We see ourselves as internally defective, woefully undisciplined or worse. We attempt to hide our pain by lying to ourselves and others. As a result, we live a double life.

"There is nothing more genuine than breaking away from the chorus to learn the sound of your own voice," declares Po Bronson.

Trapped between a belief about who we are *supposed* to be, and who we *really* are, our growth becomes stunted; we live in conflict and become indecisive; our energy is fragmented; and we are thus rendered ineffective.

Anytime we act like somebody that we are not, it strips our vital energy, creativity and confidence.

I love the way that neuroscientist, author and speaker, Dr. Caroline Leaf (2009, pp. 11), put it, "You can only be you. Who you are at the core will leak-out, no matter how much you suppress it. . . . In order to sustain a consistent outlook and pattern, your thoughts, your words, your spirit, and your actions must line-up. That means when you say something that your brain doesn't 'believe' – if your statement isn't part of you on a cellular level – it is unsustainable."

If you happen to be a student who is feeling this way, then you desperately need to get to the point where you say, "Enough is enough! No longer will I live my life according to other peoples' expectations. No longer will I define who I am by the measuring rods of others. Instead, I will determine the parameters of my life's story and success."

Dr. Leaf (2009, pp. 12) continues, "Your own gift is more than enough, and once you uncover that gift and its structure, you can walk in freedom, knowing yours is unlike anyone else's. . . . Your life experiences, the lessons you've learned, and your unique gift all combine, giving you the opportunity to walk into the future with unlimited potential to grow into your own success."

So, what is the bottom line of all of this? It's that you are unique, special and gifted to contribute to the world and those around you in amazing ways. And it is my hope that this book will assist you toward this realization.

Additional cognitive hot spots experienced by students include: alcohol & drug abuse and addiction, fear, perfectionism, self-sabotage, and the victim mentality. These are reviewed in significant detail in my 2011 book entitled, *I've Fallen and I Can Get Up! - The Ultimate Life Recovery Program.* These all represent cognitive baggage that must be cleared away. Additionally, they are reviewed as a part of the *Get Up! College* class & boot camp curriculum, the foundation upon which this book is based.

CHAPTER SEVEN

EMOTIONAL FACTORS IN COGNITION

Emotion turning back on itself, and not leading on to thought or action, is the element of madness.

-John Sterling

The word "emotion" is derived from the Latin "emovere" – "e" suggests "away" and "movere" is to "move"—more fully meaning "to move out of or to agitate." The root of this word is closely tied to motivation. And both indicate action.

Researcher Howard (1986) writes, "Such action is related to an individual's goals, so that essentially, motivation is action in pursuit of a goal." And since emotion is action resulting from circumstances that either enhance or threaten a goal, to the degree that I am positively motivated, I am pursuing a goal; to the degree that I am emotionally negative, I perceive a threat to my goal.

"So, what does this mean to me as a student?" you might ask.

Well, it simply demonstrates the effects of motivation and goals on your emotional state of mind. More specifically, it serves to highlight action versus inaction—that of powerfulness in happily, successfully and confidently moving toward your goals. Or conversely, "powerlessness"—generating fear and emotional negativity often manifest by anxiety and depression whenever you are disconnected from what it is that you truly want for your life.

For now, what is important is that you understand the interrelationship of thoughts and behavior and emotions. Because, further down the road when we transition into developing an academic and life success blueprint, this information will help bridge the social, cognitive and goals portion of this books' strategies for success.

And by the way, we'll review more about social support in Part Four when I describe the *Get Up! College* boot camp and how it all works. For now we're focusing on cognition and goals so that you can begin to apply this information to your life, beginning right now.

Says Joseph Ledoux,

> *The first funeral I ever attended was also my first introduction to the fragrance of gardenias. The nearness of gardenias still filters an event with a melancholy element.*

Now, to further illustrate how our emotions affect our thought processes, I'd like to share a practical, day-to-day scenario from the life of a student, "Emily."

Emily is an eighteen year old student attending a midsized college in Southern California. Let's see if you can personally identify with some of what occurred with regards to Emily's thoughts and mood as you listen to her story:

Emily walks into class ten minutes early, hoping to check her answers to an "open book & collaborative" homework assignment prior to handing it in to her professor. Upon entering the classroom, she immediately detects a whiff of the very cologne that her recently ex-boyfriend frequently wears. It is permeating the air.

Her fellow student, Allen, has apparently discovered a passion for this brand of cologne and wears it with pride. And he wears lots of it! (And no, it's not Old Spice!)

Allen likely has no idea that Emily's ex-boyfriend absolutely loves this brand of cologne (We'll say it's Wall Street by Bond No. 9, CK One or Guess for Men—my personal favs.!) and wore it almost constantly while they were dating. Unfortunately, her ex-boyfriend was cruelly abusive to her and she has suffered emotionally all this past year as a result.

Now, upon smelling the cologne (something quite benign), her mind quickly goes to unpleasant memories of her ex-. Suddenly, her brain has started to connect the smell of the cologne with painful memory branches and negative thought clusters formerly lying dormant within the neural circuitry of her brain.

Emily proceeds to ask a fellow student to review the homework study helps with her, when suddenly she experiences a flood of negative thoughts and emotions. Her mood is now beginning to slip.

Before entering the classroom, Emily, totally ready to start the day with "Mocha Frapp" in hand and all, was having a good morning, but now her senses are starting to connect with neuronal branches of prior sensory experiences related to her ex-boyfriend and the abuse that she suffered. And like a pinball, her thoughts now ricochet from memory to memory and from thought cluster to thought cluster. In fact, her brain is becoming saturated with negativity and she feels herself becoming depressed.

You might ask, "All of this because of the smell of cologne?" Yes! This is an example of just how easily negative thoughts can be produced when one of our senses makes even an innocent connection with a painful or negative memory.

But hang on a second, a moment of choice now emerges. There is still hope for a positive outcome for Emily. The brain sends and receives chemicals through what are called, "brain synapses." Neuroscientists often refer to brain synapses as the point wherein choices are made.

At the moment of choice, the synapse will activate an electrochemical reaction in accordance with a choice, thought or interpretation of an event. A positive choice, thought or interpretation increases the likelihood of a balanced, and therefore, positive electrochemical reaction—which assists in forming new, healthy neuronal tree branches—adding health to the "forest" of the brain. Conversely, a negative choice, thought or interpretation releases an unbalanced, and therefore, negative electrochemical reaction—which assists in forming new, unhealthy neuronal tree branches—adding "toxicity" to the "forest" of the brain.

Emily can now choose to allow the negative downward slide, or she can choose to counteract it by checking in (even if via text or a quick call) with a trusted friend (social support) or via positivity (cognitive support) by rehearsing the truth about who she really is—her goals, potential and enormous value as a young woman. In fact, now would be a fantastic time for Emily to Challenge Distorted Beliefs (CDB) and/or recite Personal Positive Affirmations (PPA) and/or practice Automatic Negative Thought Stopping (ANTS)—three powerful exercises that will be reviewed more extensively in Chapter Nine.

Now catch this (this is where cognitive resilience training meets day-to-day life): if she chooses to counteract the negativity, then healthier branches related to her past will begin to form, essentially melting away, into gas literally (no kidding!), the negative thought clusters over time. The choice is now hers.

Hopefully you can now begin to see how forming an abundance of healthy neuronal "trees of the mind"—kind of like cellular networks—can have a compounding effect. It assists students with the resources to increase the likelihood of interpreting daily events in a more positive way.

And when students engage in such cognitive resilience exercises in a small group or mentor led classroom setting (can someone say, "dynamic and powerful social support!"?), as will be discussed in Part Four, then cognitive resilience really comes *alive* (and "b-t-dubs," students' sense of hope does too)!

> *We need eleven positive thoughts to balance one negative thought.*

> -Albert Einstein

Well, as we have seen thus far, there are many potential pitfalls that can drag students down. But the good news remains that there are some amazing strategies and techniques that students can use to successfully navigate around and through them.

The following chapters will provide practical application of what you are learning, so that by following the exercises contained, you can knock out *your* cognitive hot spots and move forward toward becoming more of the student you are meant to be—positive, effective, confident and more fully *alive*!

CHAPTER EIGHT

COGNITIVE HD

The mind is its own place, and in itself can make a Heaven or Hell.

-John Milton, Paradise Lost

The brain is a complex and highly sophisticated machine, arguably the most awesome of all human organs.

Its physical consistency is likened to that of custard. In fact, a living brain is so soft that it can be cut with a butter knife. But, please don't try this at home!

The brain weighs approximately 3 lbs.

Brain neurons are typically the oldest cells in your body.

A newborn brain contains something on the order of 100 billion nerve cells. That is most of the neurons a brain will ever have.

And did you know that brain neurons happen to be the longest cells in your body? In some cases a neuron may be up to 3 feet long. Perhaps that's why some people say, "A little knowledge goes a long way!"

The brain's various parts and its nerve cells are connected by nearly 1 million miles of nerve fibers. The human brain has the largest area of uncommitted cortex (with no specific function identified so far) of any species on earth. This gives humans extraordinary flexibility for learning.

The brain is powerful. The fact is, however, we only tap into approximately 2-3% of its raw power.

The brain is dynamic. It is ever adapting in response to new stimuli introduced daily through the five senses.

The pioneering neurophysiologist Sir Charles Sherrington, in an oft' quoted passage, describes the brain this way: "It is as if the Milky Way entered upon some cosmic dance. Swiftly, the brain becomes an enchanted loom where millions of flashing shuttles weave a dissolving pattern, always a meaningful pattern, though never an abiding one—a shifting harmony of sub-patterns."

Indeed, the brain is an amazing organ! That is why understanding the internal dynamics of brain change serves as an important prelude to applying the *Get Up! College* strategies as outlined in the following chapters.

Since the brain is adaptable and changeable, the term "plastic" is a fitting descriptor—the understanding of which presents both a privilege and a responsibility. It represents a privilege because it invites an individual to strive to become all that he or she can be, regardless of the past. It also presents an opportunity for a student to overhaul his or her life and to develop into his or her unique gift to the world. It represents a responsibility because the potential for negative development exists as well—what is often called in the field of neuroscience, "the paradox of plasticity."

The paradox of plasticity recognizes that just as positive changes in your brain can be made through positive thoughts, desires, choices and actions, so negative changes can be established just the same. Therefore, you do well to daily consider the results of your choices on the development of your brain—especially since every habit, thought and experience becomes a very real, physical part, of you.

Have you ever asked yourself the question, *What is it that I truly want out of my studies?* Do you want an increased sense of personal effectiveness in impacting the world around you; a clear career pathway; high earning potential; friends with whom you can form a life and career enriching network; a more positive attitude; increased wisdom, knowledge or learning potential; better time and money management skills; freedom from poverty; or to perhaps find a mate? The good news is that truly anything you desire out of your time in college, and want seriously enough, is possible to you.

The choice is yours.

> *Your time is limited, don't waste it living someone else's life . . .*
> *Have the courage to follow your heart and intuition, they*

somehow know what you truly want to become. Everything else is secondary.

-Steve Jobs

As alluded to earlier, the brain has a built in "search and destroy" mechanism (SDM) that operates to both manage and destroy "toxic" and negative thoughts. Since thoughts grow branches and multiply in kind, they eventually become grouped or clustered together, much like telecommunications or computer cluster networks. A conglomeration of negative thoughts adversely influence ones attitude, behavior and emotions.

According to Dr. Caroline Leaf (2010), "We have billions of existing thought clusters with their emotions attached giving their specific attitude or 'flavor' . . . and every type of emotion has one of only two roots – love or fear. Love and fear are the root emotions and all other emotions grow from these."

She further contends, "Science is showing us there is a massive 'unlearning' of negative toxic thoughts when we operate in love. The brain releases a chemical called oxytocin, which literally melts away the negative toxic thought clusters, so that rewiring of new nontoxic circuits can happen. This chemical also flows when we trust and bond and reach out to others. Love literally wipes out fear."

Consider this for a moment: if everything in your life can be boiled down to either love or fear, would this not help simplify matters a great deal? If you came to understand your toxic thoughts as stemming from fear, would this not present an opportunity to grasp a better handle on your life and what may be driving you?

Conversely, since love, as manifest by nurturing oneself and others, showing patience and kindness, making healthy life decisions or offering a gentle touch to someone in need, actually has a healthy effect on your brain, doesn't this sound like an attractive way to restructure your thinking and begin to transform your life?

Besides oxytocin, other electro chemicals, such as dopamine, give us a positive "charge" whenever we anticipate something favorable or become excited in a positive way. Such electro chemicals have a positive impact on our thoughts, motivation levels and mental makeup.

Additionally, serotonin and a few other chemicals are essential components of a loving, positive, stable and optimally functioning brain.

It's amazing to think that electro chemicals, activated by making healthy and loving choices, and by social connectedness, can actually trigger search and destroy mechanisms that literally melt away negative thoughts— further highlighting the power of the social component of the *Get Up! College* strategies for success.

Now, bear in mind, the brain's search and destroy mechanism is only effective to the degree that it has enough healthy neuronal trees and branches to accomplish the mission efficiently. This is primarily because if the negativity is intense enough, that is, if there is an overabundance of unhealthy neuronal branches and trees when compared with that of healthy neuronal branches and trees, then the healthy neurons that *do* exist are over taxed and electrochemically become imbalanced, resulting in decreased efficiency, and therefore, diminished effectiveness of this search and destroy mechanism.

This depletion of available resources and energy that might otherwise be used for other important functions results in anxiety, depression, fatigue, diminished concentration and stress overwhelm.

This is precisely why students with an unhealthy mindset are tired a good part of the time. It is a lot of work to try and manage toxic trees and branches.

And socially speaking, students with depleted cognitive function often report a decrease in personal confidence, exuberance, memory, spontaneity and present mindedness—often failing to remain "in the moment."

That is because resources are being diverted to manage negative thoughts and are creating disorganized electrochemical reactions within the brain, resulting in confusion and a restriction of freedom to more fully engage in a socially meaningful way.

Similar dynamics hold true in relation to physical health, academic and professional pursuits. The result is a decreased quality of performance, and therefore, a decreased quality of life.

Since each nerve cell in your brain looks like a tree with a central cell body and branches, a leading researcher at the University of California at Berkeley, Marion Diamond, together with an award winning science writer, Janet Hopson, refer to neuronal branches as, "the magic trees of the mind."

Dr. Leaf, in a 2010 interview with marketing expert, entrepreneur, and success coach, Ali Brown, enhanced my understanding of the trees of the mind by offering a colorful analogy. She referred to healthy trees of the mind as, "green trees," and toxic trees of the mind as, "black trees."

Dr. Leaf explained that on a microscopic level, neuronal trees and branches have a unique appearance similar to what we might see in a forest when comparing a healthy and vibrant green tree to that of a tree that is dying. She teaches that green trees represent love, while black trees represent fear, and that, "We are wired to build green trees. . . . We are wired for love. . . . The black trees are hijackers. They are not supposed to be there. This is not according to God's order and design."

She asserted that issues such as forgiveness and un-forgiveness build physically into the brain, and that we can choose to build in a positive or a negative direction.

Furthermore, said Leaf, "'I can't' is not neutral. . . . It's a decision. And the decision to tap into the 'I can' destroys [melts away into gas] black trees," thus fostering the development of green trees.

So what is the result of this dynamic process? A new green tree thought strand begins to enhance one's ability to operate from love, as opposed to fear.

I have referred to Dr. Leaf's illustration of the green and black trees in work with my clients and in workshops where I have presented on the topic of cleansing toxic thoughts. The audience catches the concept almost immediately. They absolutely love it.

Should my students find themselves becoming stuck and feeling negative, overly stressed or defeated, I often remind them, "Keep planting that forest of green trees." Almost without fail I will get a call or text some time later, saying, "Thank you! What you said really helped. Things got better after you reminded me to keep planting green trees."

> *The brain is the violin and the soul is the violinist. They both need to work together in order to make beautiful music.*
>
> -Father Charles Ara

Something that I learned while training in hypnosis, and in research on the subject of cognitive change processes and psychotherapy, is the fact that the moment a memory moves from the unconscious to the conscious mind, it can be changed. This is where a window of opportunity exists for reconsolidation to take place, as new proteins are formed following retrieval.

The goal of therapy is to help a client recall troubling and unresolved memories, and then to reorganize such memories in a healthier way. And while there are a variety of techniques to accomplish this, we will review many of the most essential strategies as we move along through the book.

And perhaps the greatest thing about many cognitive exercises is their transportability, in that, students can practice many of them on the go, thus fortifying the mind against the many stressors that life as a college student can bring. They're really quite easy to use.

Ultimately, regardless of the program or technique that an agent of change (a coach, counselor, teacher or therapist) may use to foster strength and resilience in your life, the element of human interaction is typically what ultimately provides the healing balm. That is why I am such a big proponent of individual therapy, one-to-one mentoring and group interaction within a classroom or similar setting (a statement that may appear to be at odds with prior statements I have made wherein I expressed the need for counselors and therapists to get out of the office and into the community or onto the college campus). However, these statements are entirely compatible, as there is a time and place for both. But, oftentimes we don't avail ourselves of the opportunity to work with others.

In our Western culture, we have a tendency to believe that we cannot allow others to know us for who we really are. We hide behind a façade of who we think we are supposed to be. After all, we think we must be strong and "have it all together." And again I say, this is especially true for students from Middle Eastern, Asian, and otherwise dogmatic religious communities, wherein bringing shame upon members of one's family or community is oftentimes frowned upon.

If this all sounds familiar, then I urge you to advocate for a *Get Up! College* class on your campus, wherein students can share their humanness, pain, struggles, disappointments and failures in a safe atmosphere of commonality and acceptance.

For some, this is an incredibly freeing and important step toward experiencing true intimacy and the psychological wellbeing that only human connection can give. Students who have a need for more intensive work, such as, psychotherapy, can then be referred by the class facilitator. In this way, the *Get Up! College* class facilitator serves as a safety net for students who might otherwise "fall through the cracks."

Albert Einstein is also quoted as having said, "Amidst difficulty lies opportunity."

Decide at this moment to seize opportunity by taking personal responsibility for growing *through* your present difficulties. Chances are that many of your difficulties are the fruit of a toxic mind established over many years. Begin now to establish a healthy state of mind.

Get with a therapist and/or join a small group or the *Get Up! College* success boot camp or class and do the work required to begin reprogramming the toxic thoughts that have held you captive and which contribute to fear, confusion and self-sabotage of your life and college experience. Your new mentality will forge a pathway to greater mental clarity, unbridled personal growth and life and academic success.

And as we move through the remainder of this book, start thinking about how the information presented thus far can be applied to your life.

Remember, cognition will ultimately pair with social support and goals, creating a synergistic explosion of healthy trees of the mind and a more focused, positive and powerful life direction. So stay tuned!

COGNITIVE BOOTCAMP

Don't ever think you cannot do it. Don't ever hate your upbringing. The cards you were dealt become your unique story. The more difficult the journey, the more interesting and powerful you will become. Great stories are formed at the end of great difficulty.

-Dr. Chris

Arriving now at Chapter Nine, you have already been introduced to the concept of brain plasticity, that is, brain changeability, adaptability and modifiability—the "Abilities"—pleasure to meet you! Also, you have explored the concept of personal growth and transformation via the *Get Up! College* formula for success.

And by this point in the book, maybe you've even identified the cognitive hot spots responsible for sabotaging your personal progress thus far. Remember, the power of choice, that is, the ability to alter your life's destiny, is yours for the taking. So, with this understanding in mind, you are now well positioned to focus on the techniques that will help you apply what you have learned thus far.

Now, I made the decision to include the cognitive hot spots in the aforementioned chapter as a prelude to the goals portion that we will get into a bit further down the road, namely because I have come to understand the absolute necessity of healthy cognition as a prelude to success. And also because I realize that fear of the unknown (aka, "the mysteries of the mind") often blinds our ability to see that change is indeed possible. It is quite natural to become frozen with fear in the face of the unfamiliar, leaving the fog of confusion to maintain its stifling grip over our lives.

That is why it is often said that "knowledge is power." This is especially true when dealing with the underlying dynamics that influence our thoughts, feelings and behavior. In fact, by being armed with this book's knowledge about the mind, we come to see that it is really quite simple to apply the *Get Up! College* strategies and techniques—all in preparation toward establishing a blueprint for academic and life success—which the following exercises build into. And this is no small matter.

Even as I write this book, I am well aware that some will pass it off as "too deep" or "too clinical." Instead, some will prefer material that merely puts a Band Aid on their problems or simply makes them feel better.

However, the reality is that to self-architect significant change in your life is serious business. And if you are willing to work for it, then the sky's the limit on who and what you can become. And why not? After all, you only live once. So, why not go for it? At least, that's my thinking.

Dr. Daniel Amen (2002), clinical neuroscientist, psychiatrist and medical director of the Amen Clinics writes that "Optimizing your life has a positive impact on brain function. As brain function impacts behavior, so too does behavior impact the brain. There is scientific evidence that living a positive and spiritual life improves brain function. As with computers, hardware problems in the brain can be helped by special programming techniques or software."

That is why in the following, we will review some of the very best techniques—many of which can be practiced in the comfort of home.

The Magic Pill Technique

The "Magic Pill" technique is something that I learned in graduate school. It invites you to answer the following question (by writing it on a piece of paper): If you could take a magic pill that would resolve all of your life's troubles and worries, and then wake to find that somehow everything is brand new, what would be different? This clarifying exercise is similar to the Major Definite Purpose question that will be introduced a bit further along.

I really like the Magic Pill exercise because it provides an organized way to get in touch with what is weighing on a person, what is holding him or her back and where it hurts. And this is crucial.

Any time we have an opportunity to bring our cares and concerns from deep within where we can better express, understand and organize them, we have already won half of the battle. In my work over the years, I have discovered that people sometimes feel anxious and depressed, but haven't the faintest clue as to why.

Inviting disappointments, fears and painful memories to emerge from the unconscious and subconscious minds to the conscious mind will provide you with an opportunity to confront and process cognitive toxicity in an intentional, healthy and solution-oriented way.

When you ask yourself the Magic Pill question, you may be surprised at what surfaces. Oh, and by the way, this exercise also provides a perfect platform for discussion among peers in a classroom or small group setting.

You will want to write your response(s) on a clean sheet of paper. By writing things down, not only are you able to actually see what is ailing you, but you then have the added benefit of releasing it from your mind, thus getting it out onto paper. This is a tremendously freeing exercise!

Later on, while creating your blueprint for academic and life success, you will dynamically discover solutions to some of the more perplexing issues facing you at the present time. This is where mountains that seem to loom like giants before you will begin to dissolve as a result of the positivity being built into your life. Pretty cool, huh?

One Page Miracle for the Soul

The second technique shared by Dr. Amen in his book, *Healing the Hardware of the Soul* (don't you just love that title?!), is the One Page Miracle for the Soul exercise.

At the top of a clean sheet of paper write, What do I really want? and What am I doing to make it happen?

Then, in *four* separate categories write the following:

1) Relationships

Campus Organizations I Would Like to Join:

Girlfriend, Spouse or Lover:

Children:

Friends:

Family:

The second category relates to School, Profession and Finances. Under this category you will want to list:

2) Academic, Career, and Finance Goals

Long Term & Short Term Academic Goals:

Long Term & Short Term Career Goals:

And finally,

Long Term & Short Term Financial Goals:

3) Under the third category, that of self, write:

Physical Goals:

Emotional Goals:

And,

Personal Interests:

4) Then finally, Soul.

Under this heading you will want to write

Spirit:

Relationship with God:

And,

Character & Personality Development:

According to Dr. Amen, this exercise enhances prefrontal cortex functioning by helping you focus on eternal values for your life. It also allows you to see beyond the moment and plan for the future, enhancing decision-making ability and judgment. This assists in avoiding impulsive, destructive and potentially life-altering decisions.

The One Page Miracle for the Soul also helps you feel focused, organized and hopeful more quickly than almost any other exercise of which I am personally aware.

You may want to start by first writing, on a separate sheet of paper, your values for each category. For example, Academic Excellence; Developing Strong Social Skills; Remaining Physically Fit; Networking with Student Peers; Always Working with a Mentor; Personal Wisdom; Wealth; Fulfilling Relationships; Fame; Personal Accomplishments; Leaving a Legacy; Honesty and Integrity; Faith in Yourself; Faith in a Higher Power; and How You Appear to Others. Then write down what you are doing *right now* to accomplish these important items that you have placed on your list.

I still recall several years ago when I personally completed this exercise. It had a powerful impact on my life. I still carry the paper from that original exercise. It is laminated and remains in my wallet at all times. I review it daily before leaving the house, then again at night before going to bed, and sometimes even when waiting for something or someone while I'm out running errands.

> *Whatever is true, whatever is noble, whatever is right, whatever is pure, whatever is lovely, whatever is admirable—if anything is excellent or praiseworthy—think about such things.*
>
> -The Scriptures

The next exercise we will review is called *Challenging Distorted Thoughts and Beliefs (CDB)*.

This is a simple and easy to use technique. It simply means that you become more aware of your thoughts, rather than just passively receiving whatever comes to mind. This way you can better decide if your thoughts are true or not, and you can either accept or reject them, based on reality and *not* on distorted thinking. For example, if while practicing this exercise a thought emerges that is untrue, then it can be rejected immediately. In its place you might say, "I reject this A, B, C thought, and instead I accept X, Y and Z as true."

In time, a person can really have fun with this exercise in order to further reinforce positivity. It's great when you get to the point where you can actually play with or even chuckle at the negative thoughts that use to weight you down.

This exercise is further enhanced when an individual is a participant in either personal cognitive therapy, a cognitive therapy process group or a classroom wherein fellow students can open up and share common struggles. A good cognitive therapist or savvy group or classroom leader can promote valuable feedback, thus enabling students to better analyze thoughts and beliefs.

Men are not disturbed by things, but the view they take of things.

-Epictetus, 55-135 A.D.

Automatic Negative Thought Stopping (ANTS)

The term ANT is an acronym for Automatic Negative Thoughts. These are thoughts that just appear seemingly from out of nowhere and seek to pervade a person's thoughts. They come in a variety of forms and are invasive. In fact, as stated earlier, "They really know how to eat your lunch if you let them!"

ANT's include:

Blaming - and failing to take personal responsibility.

Overgeneralizing - such as "always" and "never" thinking.

Mindreading - assuming that someone is thinking the worst about you or must be upset, angry or disappointed because he or she failed to greet, acknowledge or react to you in a way you think they should.

Fortunetelling - assuming things will work out for the worst.

Disproportionate Self-Blame - criticizing and blaming oneself for even the slightest imperfection or infraction.

Thinking with Your Feelings - we alluded to this in an earlier chapter.

Automatic Negative Thought Stopping (now adding the "S" at the end to make "ANTS") is the remedy for negative, intrusive or overly emotion-laden thoughts. ANTS exercises can easily be done at home and are to be practiced daily by students who are serious about increasing cognitive resilience.

Every time a negative thought appears or you feel yourself heading down the "slippery slope" of negativity, simply stop the thought, switch your thinking to something more positive and counteract the negativity with the truth of the matter.

For instance, ladies, suppose you are walking across campus and you see a poster with a picture of a scantily clad and attractive young woman appearing to have all of the guys on campus at her fingertips. Your mind could potentially think, *I will never be that beautiful. I will never be able to attract a man. I am destined to a life of endless term papers and just "chillin" with the girls. After all, no guy will ever want to be with me!*

Then, as if your thoughts were not already bad enough, your mind switches to recount all your past failures, and suddenly your mood begins to spiral DOWN, DOwn, *down*. "Haagen-Dazs anyone?"

This represents a bad case of ANT invasion!

In response, you can open up a can of "Whoop ANT Repellant!"—hopefully, immediately upon the initial thought entering your mind—by saying to yourself, "I am beautiful just the way I am. God made me unique and special for just the right guy. Besides, I am in control of my body, and if I choose to enhance my appearance in some way, then I can and I will. I am capable of obtaining whatever it is that I truly want. I will be successful."

A sense of excitement will oftentimes kick in as you begin to plot just exactly how you are going to go about achieving your objectives for success in this area of your life. This is far better than the alternative, and more accurately represents the truth. Wouldn't you agree?

Students of mine who struggle with negative thoughts (and most of us do at times) are often asked to create a list of personal strengths identifying five, ten or fifteen personal attributes that they will review on a daily basis. This way, their ANT repellant is always on the ready.

I have even worked with students over the years who have confessed, "I cannot think of anything good about myself." Together, we have no problem finding plenty of good things to add to their list.

Besides, even if you do not believe the truth about yourself, the subconscious mind does not discriminate between truth and non-truth (isn't that cool?), but simply logs input, stores it as true, and voila!—a new healthy mind branch can still be formed within the neuronal circuitry of your brain. Remember, there is nothing either good or bad (well, not really, but that's a whole different philosophical and/or theological conversation), but thinking makes it so.

Positive Affirmations (PA), Positive Personal Affirmations (PPA) and Positive Personal and Peer Affirmations (PPPA)

Positive affirmations are powerful. This is a quick, daily routine that works wonders in terms of developing a healthy mind forest and building personal confidence.

I've made the habit of reading a list of positive affirmations every morning before I leave for work as part of my daily routine, and then again each night before going to bed.

Again, a positive affirmations list is simply a list of five, ten or fifteen positive things about yourself that you can say (out loud whenever possible) on a routine basis to send positive messages to your subconscious mind.

We all have mornings that we awake and something is weighing us down. We feel tired or something particularly negative greets us before we even have a chance to hit Starbucks! It may be the overwhelming thought of a test for which we know we did not adequately prepare.

I recall having such a morning several weeks ago. I was wrestling with all the demands of the day and my mind was tempted to rehearse those areas where things may not be exactly as I would have them to be, *yet*.

Then I whipped out my positive affirmations, together with my goals and daily priority list, and reviewed them as I was getting ready to head to a campus to speak. Within minutes my attitude shifted, and I left the house that morning feeling confident and filled with possibility, as if standing in direct defiance of anything that would even dare to get in my way.

Since positive affirmations build healthy tree branches in the forest of the mind, they are a great gift releaser. Every time we affirm a positive attribute in ourselves, our unique ability is further strengthened. This is fantastic, as it puts us in touch with our personal gifts and brings them top of mind where we can more readily position ourselves to operate from a place of strength, as opposed to operating from a position of weakness or personal vulnerability.

I am currently working with a freshman college student who is constantly reminded of his personal inadequacies every time he reports to work. And he needs this job because he helps his family by paying most of his own tuition, room and board.

And although he tries to ignore the well-positioned jabs of criticism by his peers, eventually the tension builds to the point that he verbally explodes. And it's not pretty, let me tell you!

I told him, "It's not enough to simply ignore the jabs, but you must build the positive scaffolds of your mind by rehearsing the truth about yourself so intensively, and with such determination (through positive affirmations), that your gifts and the truth about yourself are top of mind at all times. In this way, you will not merely ignore the jabs, but will also be empowered, equipped and imbued with the mental clarity and vigor necessary to better evaluate them.

By maintaining a powerful force of truth and positive energy in your mind, you will more readily identify the negativity for what it is, and therefore, become empowered to respond in a constructive way.

As you become increasingly capable of more accurately discerning between destructive criticism and constructive peer feedback, you will become better able to learn and grow into your role as both a student and budding professional.

As knowledge builds upon knowledge, your gifts and creative genius will emerge stronger unto *automaticity* (when we master something so well that we can do it as second nature or automatically), your confidence will grow and you will stop second guessing your performance all of the time."

I told him this because academically, professionally and personally we are not meant to come from a position of weakness, such as when we second guess ourselves. Instead, we are meant to operate increasingly from a position of strength. That's how we are wired. That is precisely why high school and college students should learn from the very get-go to capitalize on these brain fortifying techniques.

Build positive affirmations into your daily routine. You will be amazed at the difference it makes. That is likely why someone once said, "I would rather go a morning without breakfast than a morning without positive affirmations."

Additional techniques, such as *Deep Breathing Exercises* and *Journaling* are further discussed in some detail as a part of the *Get Up! College* boot camp and classes.

And finally, that of *Healing Painful Memories* can be vitally important for some students, particularly for victims of abuse. This is best done with a trained therapist because it requires skilled guidance for maximum benefit and safety.

Also, the nurturing quality of the therapist often plays a crucial role in the healing process, as illustrated in the case of Anil (reviewed in this book's Part Two, The Message).

And again, this is where a *Get Up! College* boot camp or on campus class can play a valuable role by acting as a safety net in referring students who are in particular need of more in-depth therapy.

A skilled facilitator can also conduct small groups, facilitate safe and meaningful classroom discussion (wherein students learn they are not alone) and provide one-to-one student support.

CHAPTER TEN

GRADUATING COGNITIVE BOOTCAMP

Congratulations! You are now officially a graduate of the *Get Up! College* cognitive boot camp. With your new cognitive mind care strategies fully in place, you are ready to embark on the next leg of this exciting journey—a journey filled with exciting possibility, adventure and discovery. This is where the cognitive portion of the *Get Up! College* formula naturally transitions into the goals portion. So get ready to launch as never before!

Thus far, you have learned many things about the mind related to the importance of strengthening cognitive resilience. And as we begin the next part of the book, you will discover how robust cognition empowers you to more readily envision, step into and realize your academic and personal goals. Conversely, you will notice how goals serve to increase cognitive clarity and strength, as each dynamically amplifies the other.

And of course, the social component of the *Get Up! College* program is deeply anchored by the classroom and boot camp style through which it is delivered, as we'll discuss a bit further along.

We have already reviewed what neuroscientists are saying about neuroplasticity and the potential for the brain to change and adapt. *Get Up! College* is further supported by scientific discoveries related to the systemic nature of various aspects of our universe, from micro to macro systems, insofar as change in one component of a system often results in changes to other components as well. This information proves especially useful in highlighting the dynamic, synergistic and compounding power of the *Get Up! College* formula as we shift into the following chapters.

It is my hope that as you read, you will continue to work through and apply the exercises diligently. If you are at all like me, you may have a tendency to skip over them, preferring instead to simply read the book's contents.

A Word of Caution: The power of *Get Up! College* lies in the practical application of the knowledge presented. So please do not skip any of the exercises, as these will assist you in applying what you are learning. To the degree that you apply this formula, you will grow and progress as a strong, resilient and confident student.

Ask yourself the following questions:

What have I learned thus far about my thoughts and how my brain works?

And,

What are some areas of my life wherein I have been held back from growing because of distorted thinking (with regard to academics, finances, social relationships, time management or transition to college related stressors)?

And,

Which of the cognitive exercises did I find especially helpful?

And finally,

How can I apply what I am learning in this book to my academic and personal life, beginning right now?

I am rooting for you as you embark on this next step toward wholeness and academic and life success!

PART FOUR

PART FOUR

CHAPTER ELEVEN

G-FORCE

Success is goals. The rest is commentary.

-Brian Tracy

In this chapter your new cognitive mindset (which you recall from prior chapters deals more with the *conscious mind*) converges with the power of goals. Goals of course have somewhat more to do with your *subconscious mind*, for example, intuition, emotion and inspiration. The result is the dynamic integration of two distinct, yet interrelated, elements of *you*.

You will begin to discover that strong and clear cognition clears the runway of your mind, while goals tap into your motivation, resulting in the dynamic and life changing force that is *Get Up! College.*

While I do not know the particulars of your situation and what it is that you may be presently facing (for example, a botched test or nightmare professor, financial stressors, time management challenges, problems with procrastination, family troubles, problems managing the social demands that often accompany college life, work demands, struggles related to raising a child or caring for an elderly parent, self-destructive patterns of behavior - such as binging or purging, bondage to an addiction - such as alcohol or drugs, or any other number of painful and potentially devastating life challenges), nevertheless, there is one thing that I do know for sure—the past is the past, and this book can help you break free and begin rebuilding your academic future, beginning right here and now!

> *The past is a memory, the future a dream, today is a gift—that's why it's called, "the present."*

> -Unknown Author

Successful students view adversity, personal mistakes, failures and misfortune as opportunities to learn, grow and improve their methods toward achieving academic and life success. They do not give up.

Even though you may have failed a time or two (or even dozens of times!), you yourself are *not* a failure, because you are still trying hard in the push toward your goal to graduate and fulfill your life's dreams. And that is good, because knowing what you want and persevering to get it, regardless of the cost, is vitally important.

History tells us that in 168 B.C. a Roman Consul named, Gaius Popillius Laenas, drew a circular line in the sand around King Antiochus IV of the Seleucid Empire. He then commanded, "Before you cross this circle, I want you to give me a reply for the Roman Senate"—the implication was that Rome would declare war should the king step out of the circle before making a commitment to leave Egypt, immediately.

After considering his options, the king decided to withdraw (probably a very wise move, as historians tell us that defeat was all but certain), and the Romans effectively accomplished their objective without the spilling of blood.

One important key to academic and life success lies in developing the ability to "draw lines in the sand" consistent with your goals. This means strengthening your willingness to let go of the people, places and things that will potentially bring you down. These kinds of decisions and commitments require courage and decisiveness.

Perhaps you can recall the saying, "no guts, no glory!" This adage holds true especially in relationship to life decisions and the lines that must be drawn to strengthen them. Lines of decision can range from seemingly little sacrifices, such as, leaving the party at a decent hour in order to ensure proper rest for the next day's classes, to leaving behind a relationship that is unhealthy and damaging to your personal growth and academic success (though you may have to endure some tears and moments of loneliness as a down payment toward a better future reward—that of graduating with your class).

This once again begs the following central questions: What do you *truly* want for your life? If you could take that magic pill discussed in a previous chapter, and suddenly create any life that you want, what would your life look like? Would one of your desires be to live free of the cognitive hot spots that may be threatening your academic and personal success?

If so, what problems would be resolved? What would you set out to accomplish that has always been difficult for you? And finally, what kind of student and person would you like to become?

Please take a few moments to reflect on these questions. Invest whatever time is necessary to do so. It will be well worth it!

As we progress throughout the remainder of the book, some of the cognitive hot spots will likely surface in your mind. And you might ask, "Why would these emerge just as I am beginning to focus on my academic, career and life goals?"

The answer lies in the fact that they represent your former manner of living—a very real part of the way that you *use to* think about, see and do things. But don't worry. As you refer back to the previous chapter related to growing a healthy mind forest and apply the techniques so useful in destroying these cognitive stumbling blocks (while simultaneously forging ahead toward establishing a goals blueprint for academic and life success), then you will discover that the soil is beginning to loosen beneath your feet, and that what once held you back is beginning to be uprooted.

This represents *Get Up! College*, a social, cognitive and goals combination, beginning to perform its work in your life. So without further ado, let's dig into the power of goals.

So sure of the power of goals, that after years of speaking with audiences all over the world about personal transformation and life success, entrepreneur and success coach, Brian Tracy, said, "If I was only given five minutes to speak to you and I could only convey one thought that would help you to be more successful, I would tell you to write down your goals, make plans to achieve them and work on your plans every single day." He continued, "This advice, if you followed it, would be of more help to you than anything you could ever learn."

In expressing this sentiment, Brian Tracy is certainly not alone. In fact, many of the most successful people in the world, representing a broad range of endeavors, highlight the power of goals as a key component to their success.

The greatest need of the human being is to have a sense of meaning and purpose in life, expresses Neuroscientist, Psychiatrist and Holocaust Survivor, Victor Frankl.

There are many positive benefits to a goals-centered life. For instance, anticipation and curiosity, which are byproducts of goals, resulting in a positive and heightened state of vigilance. As discussed in Part Two, these states contribute to increased activity in the attentional areas of the brain, including the reticular cortex. Anticipation and curiosity are known as, "appetitive states," because they stimulate the mind's appetite. And hence, they are highly motivating.

Research shows that anticipation of receiving or achieving something positive increases the consistent transmission of neurochemical resources necessary to maintain focused attention. It is under such conditions that we are apt to thrive and be at our best.

And we see strong evidence of this expressed in the research cited toward the beginning of this book, don't we? In fact, as our research suggested, the anticipation of positive events drives up the pleasure in the brain even more than the reward itself.

And significantly, a whole "candy store" of positive attributes accompanies the goals-centered life. For instance, positive energy, personal empowerment, increased confidence, competence and inspired motivation are all additional byproducts of the goals-centered life. That is why I often describe goals as, "fuel in the engine of life," sparking increased enthusiasm, personal satisfaction and just plain old fun!

Additionally, goals are personally very anchoring, as they provide a positive and focused structure for your mind and for the direction of your life and studies. It would be more difficult to make a careless, foolish and potentially life altering decision after having first consulted your very own personal goals blueprint for life success, wouldn't it?

And finally, goals simplify.

By establishing clearly defined goals for your life ahead of time, you will not have to spend precious time and energy agonizing about every decision that comes your way. You will already have the answers.

When an opportunity presents itself, you simply compare it with your goals. If the opportunity is consistent with your goals and vision for life, then your decision is essentially already made. If not, then you can reject it without ever looking back, resulting in a definitive crispness to the way that you manage your life.

And so an important question emerges: With all of the potential benefits of goals, why do relatively few people practice them consistently, especially since the concept of goals is nothing new? In fact, goals have been written and spoken about perhaps more than any other topic of which I am aware, particularly within motivational circles.

Well, I think the answer lies in the fact that most people have a desire to be happy, but no real plan on how to get what it is they *say* they want. Therefore, desire remains nothing more than a wish, hope or dream. Wishing and hoping that things will get better is simply not enough!

Mark H. McCormack, in his book, *What They Don't Teach You at Harvard Business School,* tells of a study conducted between 1979 and 1989. At the beginning of the study, graduates of the Harvard MBA program were asked if they had clear, written goals for their future and plans on how their goals would be accomplished. As it turns out, only three percent of the graduates had written goals, while thirteen percent had goals, but not written. The remaining sample of students had no concrete goals beyond the activities of daily life.

Ten years later, the members of that same class were interviewed again, and it was revealed that those who had goals (but not written) earned twice as much money as those with no goals. And the three percent who had clear and written goals were earning (on average) *ten times* the amount of money as the other ninety-seven percent of graduates.

With such a marked difference between the relatively few students who set goals and those who do not, it really is a wonder why so few students set clear, specific, time-bound goals?

And while this has always been somewhat of a mystery to me, here I will list the reasons that I have been able to come up with thus far: first of all, most people are not trained to set goals; second, fear of failure often holds people back; third, a desire for security may be another reason (and yet, we are often reminded that, quite paradoxically, success and its accompanying security are achieved by those individuals who are willing to step out of their comfort zone and take risks); and a fourth and final reason that more people do not set goals is due to contentment with the status quo. This is merely a polite way of suggesting that people often settle for less than their personal best or have become (dare I say it?) la-la-la-lazy. Okay, I said it!

And yet, each and every one of us has a special gift, a "hidden genius" if you will. However, oftentimes this gift, this genius, remains untapped.

And as I wrote earlier, frustration, confusion and depression result to the extent that this is the case. In fact, as I wrote in my first book, *I've Fallen and I Can Get Up!* (2011, pp. 100), "Depression represents the chasm between where we find ourselves presently and where we would really like to be in our heart of hearts. That is why we must amplify our gift to the world through goals if we are to ever reach the levels of success and life satisfaction that are truly possible for us.

If you happen to be waiting for something or someone in order to begin establishing goals for your life, then only this question remains, 'For what and for whom are you waiting?' Because, the only one who can make your life happen the way you want it, is *you*!"

And what is even more puzzling, particularly in light of such promising research on the subject of goals, is why academic institutions do not foster a goals mindset as a standard part of the student curriculum and campus culture. Then again, likely that is why this book, together with the accompanying *Get Up! College* boot camps and classes, was created and is now being welcomed on campuses both large and small.

I first learned about goals through a sales trainer by the name of Mark Thomas. We all called him, "Coach." Coach had played basketball in college and was brought up through the ranks by the coach of all coaches, the late Coach John Wooden of UCLA fame.

Since Coach Wooden was known for his "basics and fundamentals" style of coaching, Mark taught his new sales staff in very much the same manner. And since Mark had managed to make a high six-figure income for many years as a sales professional, I figured he knew what he was talking about. So I listened, learned and applied all that I could.

During that time in my life (2004-2008), I learned that success is determined not so much by personal talent (although talent is certainly a factor to some degree), but rather, by setting and consistently pursuing clearly defined personal sales goals. Those who followed a plan and worked it consistently were ultimately the most successful in sales.

For instance, consider those earning two hundred thousand, three hundred thousand or even five hundred thousand dollars per year in retail sales commissions (representing the top 2 to 3 percent of sales professionals in the country). I found that they are not superstars any more than you, me or the neighbor, "Joe," who lives down the street. They simply followed superstar methods of applying relatively simple but crucial procedures in their sales game plan. They envision what they want, set goals and intensely and consistently focus on their goals.

As I studied the characteristics of some of the top retail sales producers in the nation, I quickly learned that natural talent is further down the list of success attributes than many people realize. In fact, honesty, product knowledge, attention to customer needs and wants, a personal touch and a set of clearly defined professional goals are at the very top of the list.

And having applied all that Coach taught me, I managed to more than double my income in those four years, broke numerous sales records and quickly rose to a sales manager position. I even managed to work for a national corporation wherein I was afforded a luxury personal automobile, extravagant client entertainment expense account and travels to various cities (always via limousine from the airport), including accommodations at some of the nation's finest hotels.

Truthfully, I felt as if I had gone "from rags to riches" in a relatively short period of time, and all because of the power of goals, combined with consistently working a very basic system that reflected those goals.

However, my heart was calling me back to my first love, that of speaking, counseling/coaching and writing. And fortuitously, I was able to hand off my sizeable customer following to someone I felt would take good care of "my people."

And now with some of my knowledge gaps about business and the way the world works filled-in, and being armed with a clear understanding of the power of goals, I was ready to embrace my career once again, but this time in a more intentional, and therefore, effective way.

I share this 411 about my life realizing that many students and families' lives have been overturned by the economic struggles currently facing our nation. And I wish to convey hope that there is in fact a way to successfully navigate all the economic, time management and academic challenges that often accompany student life.

I started with virtually nothing and was able to make significant strides quickly. All of this I attribute to the power of goals, together with loads of perseverance, a positive attitude and an intense desire to succeed.

> *Show me a really great triumph that is not the reward of persistence. Genius, when you look more closely at it, usually turns out to be the sum of uncommon dedication to a task.*
>
> -Orison Swett Marden

Also, I share this personal information to illustrate how virtually everything in our lives, even winding roads, can contribute toward building the foundation of our success—if we will but listen, learn and apply the lessons as we go.

And we don't have to wait to have it all figured out before getting started. The truth is, we will *never* have it all figured out. That is why Woody Allen is quoted as having said, "Eighty percent of success is just showing up." So that, much like beginning a new workout routine or dreaded homework assignment, the hardest part oftentimes is simply getting started.

Well, what about you?

What has your life been like up to this point? What experiences, victories and failures have you encountered that might serve as a foundation of wisdom toward strengthening your ability to move forward with increased power and confidence? What strengths in high school did you capitalize on in order to get unstuck or resolve a problem or challenge? You will want to focus on these strengths and list them as reference points for your positive affirmations and academic and life success blueprint.

Are you presently going through the throes of a life-altering circumstance or otherwise grueling situation? If so, are you struggling to see beyond the clouds of confusion, bitterness and despair—all in hopes of discovering a brighter tomorrow?

How can this experience, the tilling of your heart's soil, the lessons learned and the skills developed, serve as a foundation for future success? You will want to list these as well.

And dear student, if you happen to be passing through a particularly difficult period in your life right now, then consider asking yourself, Could this dark night of the soul serve as a curious beckoning, calling me to explore untapped reservoirs of possibility that have laid dormant within me all along?

In the chapter ahead you will learn one of the very best strategies for success, that of *Present Realization*. By using present realization you will learn to envision a better life and attract more of what it is that you truly want.

CHAPTER TWELVE

SEEING IS ACHIEVING

Where there is no vision, the people perish.

-Proverbs 29:18

Vision allows us to see with our mind's eye what it is that we truly want, before it becomes a reality. Some would even argue that once something is envisioned, then it *is* reality. We just need to begin walking in, talking in and making decisions in accordance with this new reality.

It's fascinating to think that at the moment we envision something with a sincerity, passion, desire and determination so strong that we will do whatever is necessary to see it manifest in the physical world, at that very moment marching orders are transmitted throughout the cosmos. Then, it is only a matter of time before we see with our own eyes that which our mind has already beheld.

Such was the case with Walt Disney when many decades ago he envisioned a family theme park that would be "the happiest place on earth." There is a sign at the Epcot Center in Orlando Florida that quotes Disney, "If you can dream it, you can do it."

Of course, at the time that he first envisioned his theme parks, it was just that, a vision. Or was it?

One of the strongest tools of which I am personally aware is what I call present realization. Present realization is when you hold a vision in your mind's eye of something that you want to manifest in your life.

It may be a material object, becoming a college graduate, obtaining your first professional job, an exciting internship, meeting that special someone and getting married, a certain lifestyle, an award or level of academic or professional achievement, a trophy for winning a prestigious event, a character quality or personality characteristic, or any number of things that you desire.

For present realization to be effective it must emanate from within. It must be something that you desire in your heart of hearts. Also, it must be intense enough to captivate your senses and occupy your thoughts.

You will see, smell, touch, taste and hear it. For example, a student aspiring to graduate with her class might visualize herself "in the zone" of peak academic performance— remaining focused, completing homework assignments on time, attending all classes and studying into the late hours of the night if that is what it takes to graduate on time.

She will feel the diploma as it is being placed into her hand, and see herself raising it high into the air. She will hear the crowd of fellow students, family members and friends as they clap wildly while chanting her name. She might even envision her parents' faces full of glee, or smell the sweet, fragrant aroma of flowers, and taste the restaurant cuisine at the after graduation reception. She will feel the intense satisfaction of forever being able to say, "I am a college graduate!" And she will envision her life richly enhanced, all because of this monumental moment in time.

The ancestor of every action is thought.

-Ralph Waldo Emerson

So what is your vision? In the next chapter you will have a chance to transplant your personal vision into your academic and goals blueprint. So why not "swing for the fence?"

For now, on a clean sheet of paper, write answers to the following questions:

What is something(s) you are currently aspiring to? And how can practicing present realization help you achieve or realize this goal(s) in your life today?

What differences can present realization make in your behavior and attitude, beginning right now?

And,

How can present realization and the power of visualization make a difference in the one thing that you presently struggle with the most?

Next, complete this present realization exercise:

Envision one thing that you really want to see manifest in your life. Allow sufficient time for your mind to see, hear, smell, touch and/or taste the accomplishing of the goal.

(Please be sure to write your feelings and observations.)

Buddha declared, "All that we are is the result of what we have thought."

And finally, in relationship to obtaining more of what it is that you truly want, it is vitally important to be mindful of with whom and where you spend your time. Negative people, places and things will drain your vital energy and desire for success. Additionally, negative people will be prone to jealously criticize your progress.

On the other hand, positive people, places and things will fuel your energy and increase your desire for success.

> *To stimulate men and women to the discovery and perception of the truth—that they themselves are makers of themselves by virtue of the thoughts which they choose and encourage; that mind is the master weaver, both of the inner garment of*

character and the outer garment of circumstance, and that, as they may have hitherto woven in ignorance and pain they may now weave in enlightenment and happiness.

-Unknown Author

CHAPTER THIRTEEN

SO WHAT'CHA WANT?

So What'cha Want?

-Beastie Boys

In a previous chapter we reviewed the many positive benefits of goals. In this chapter we will journey through a series of potentially life-transforming exercises to help you get started with your new goals mindset and blueprint for success.

But first,

A Word of Caution: if you embrace and utilize the concepts and exercises laid out in this chapter, you will likely never be the same. Like a jet speeding down the runway, your life will rapidly accelerate toward your true passion and purpose for living. So wear your seatbelt! Friends and family will stand amazed as they witness this awe-inspiring transformation taking shape.

And forward acceleration of your life at this point in time just may not be such a bad idea. I write this because the price of continuing to live in a haphazard manner is far too high!

Now consider this: it used to be that if you were socioeconomically middle class, you could practically bump into a job with a fifty, sixty or seventy thousand dollar per year salary, and that with paid benefits.

If you managed your finances well, while this salary might not have afforded living in the lap of luxury, you could at least have lived a reasonably comfortable lifestyle, getting along pretty well. However, now with more people competing for fewer jobs, those days just may be gone, at least for the foreseeable future.

A less than impressive job outlook, combined with rising energy, food and healthcare costs, higher college and university tuition, and increased taxes represent a real wakeup call for the student planning on randomly conducting "business as usual" with regard to his or her economic future.

In, *I've Fallen and I Can Get Up!* (pp. 118), I wrote, "Economists concerns about a shrinking middle class are consistent with economic data suggesting a potentially lower quality of life for the average American earner in the years to come. Yes indeed, the days of 'just winging it' seem to be over." And now just a few short years later they *are* over!

Therefore, it is "individuals willing to create their own economic reality (entrepreneurs) through innovation, courage and creativity (fueled by clearly defined academic, career and personal life goals) who will march-forth to claim the American dream in the twenty first century" (Miller, pp. 118). Aka, you need to decide if you want to struggle financially for the rest of your life and have an increasingly diminished voice, power and influence in the world, or if you want to tap into your full potential so that you can be among those who escape the excruciating difficulties that are increasingly going to befall middle class America in the years to come. (Of course, this also depends on the kinds of leaders that we elect to serve in public office—a subject that I discuss in greater detail in my audio book, *Vote Captain US 2.0* (2014).

So students, get up and get moving. Your family and country need you. You need you!

Fortunately, getting started and creating a goals blueprint for success is not anywhere close to rocket science. In fact, it is so simple that even a child can do it. Your goals should be so clearly stated that your neighbor's eight year old child can understand exactly what it is you want and how you intend to get it.

Remember, the power of goals does not rest on the complexity of the process, but rather, on the substantial passion that you carry into the endeavor, the consistency with which you move forward and the usability (it helps if they are user friendly) of the methods employed for pursuing your goals.

In the following, let's review the very best exercises to help you get started: the first is the Magic Pill technique, as reviewed in Chapter Nine. This exercise represents a great place to start because it cuts right to the heart of what changes you would like to make in your life. It removes barriers to free thinking by suggesting that there is a magic pill that can remove anything that might even dare stand in your way.

The Magic Pill technique only requires that you have a sheet of paper, journal or notebook. The magic in this exercise is of such a powerful variety that you could even scribble it onto a napkin while dining at a local café, and by merely reviewing it daily, still achieve amazing results. For these reasons this is a great clarifying exercise. And remember, earlier we discussed the vital importance of first becoming crystal clear about what it is that you truly want before embarking.

I do suggest a notebook or some form of organizer for this and other exercises to follow, as you will want to build on these exercises in the days, weeks, months and years to come.

Next is the One Page Miracle for the Soul. This is another great exercise for helping to draw out your true values from deep within your soul.

Then, Life's Last Days question. This involves asking yourself, "If I suddenly learned that I have a terminal illness, with only a matter of days, weeks or months to live, what would I do with the remaining time?" This question will assist you toward quickly identifying your true values and what is really most important to you.

Also you can ask, "What changes will I be making?" or "What relationships will I seek to mend?" or "With whom would I like to spend a majority of my time?" or "What kind of an impact would I like to make on those closest to me?" (Perhaps there is a message that you would like to deliver to the world?)

I especially like these questions because they help put matters into proper perspective. And they are loaded with heart. For such reasons they also represent great clarifying questions. So why not consider living the rest of your life with this new mindset?

The Wish List exercise asks, "If you had no limitations at all, for example, unlimited money, time and health, then what twenty-five to fifty goals would you most like to accomplish in your life?" I like this question because it helps us tap into things we would enjoy doing, but have not paid much thought.

This is most definitely an expanding question, as it prompts an individual to think outside of the narrow confines of perceived limitations and routine thought, thus inviting exploration from a broadened perspective. With some creativity and careful consideration you will be amazed at how quickly you can come up with fifty or even a hundred things to include on your list.

Ask yourself, "What do I most enjoy doing?" and "What would I do without pay if I could only do one thing all day long?" and finally, "What am I really good at?"

While the first two questions can potentially lead a student along the path of one sided or imbalanced thinking, it would not likely be the case for very long. He or she would soon realize that whatever they determine to do must also align with their core values with regard for the whole of life. So that, endless beer parties, poker and all night raves would probably wear thin rather quickly. Besides, eventually someone will have to pay the bar tab, create a fresh round of alibis for the professor, boss or significant other, and still have the presence of mind necessary to pay the DJ :),

In all seriousness, this is another great clarifying question because it helps you identify that for which you are truly passionate and would most like to do with a good portion of your time. Again, what do you truly want for your life?

When I first created my own personal goals blueprint for life success, I followed the order of the exercises as presented above. I pondered these clarifying and expansive questions thoroughly, because I realized they serve as an important prelude to effective academic and life planning. So, be sure to follow the steps thoroughly in order to obtain the best results.

Now I invite you to begin the next phase of synthesizing your life's passions and goals into a clear and organized life success blueprint.

It is best to organize your thoughts from general to specific, from long-term goals to short-term goals—the opposite of how we typically organize our lives and daily activities.

The reason is that you will want the long-term, big picture, to inform the choices that you will make in the near future. It would make little sense to chart short-term goals before first clarifying where it is that you ultimately wish to go.

Your long-term goals should reflect your values in terms of the following: academic, career and finances; social, community and network building; character, personality and spiritual development; family; physical health and recreation; and finally, service and giving. These represent the six essential components of our lives.

After all, it is important to remain balanced. If you ignore even one major area of your life, then it is impossible to be truly whole.

And while balance may not be easy to achieve, it remains an important objective, as each component of your life is interdependent one with the other. For example, it would be unwise to tirelessly work eighty or ninety hours per week, while leaving your family, personal health and social life to suffer as a result.

After carefully considering the clarifying and expanding questions mentioned above, you will want to begin listing the long-term goals that emerge as a result of the process. I recommend combining various goals into one major goal whenever possible.

For instance, if you have long-term goals of eventually working for yourself, creating your own schedule, working from home and managing your own professional development, then you would include these under a single, major long-term goal, entitled, "I Determine My Ideal Vocation and Working Conditions." Remember, goals are best stated in the personal, positive and present tense—the "3P's." (The 3P's cements them more deeply into your subconscious mind.) The various sub-goals would then be listed beneath this one major goal, serving as a description of all that this goal entails.

The next step is to identify the specific actions necessary to achieve each long-term goal. These actions become your short-term goals and serve as stepping stones toward helping you achieve your ultimate objectives.

Examples of short-term goals, together with what is often identified as your Major Definite Purpose (or MDP), might be to obtain career counseling, conduct research to learn more about a career of interest and/or saving the money required for specialized training or business start-up costs.

If you learned that you would need several thousand dollars for training and business start-up costs, but were currently unemployed and financially broke, then your major definite purpose (defined as the one, two or three things required to "get the ball rolling" and that would have the most immediate and substantial impact on your ability to move ahead toward your other goals) would be to obtain employment in something that does not require financial capital, so that you can earn and save money as necessary to accomplish your short-term, and then eventually your long-term goals.

In addition to being clear and specific, it is important that your goals be time-bound so that your mind is alerted with an increased sense of urgency. For example, "I will obtain career counseling by such and such a date."

When a date is set, your mind—you guessed it, via your reticular cortex—is alerted and begins to focus attention toward the goal, gathering the resources necessary for the attainment of the goal. Remember, goals are meant to be accomplished. There is little value in setting goals that are unrealistic. Therefore, your goals must be achievable. Otherwise, you could become discouraged and quit.

Reflecting on the illustrations about the king and builder from an earlier chapter, we realize that we must first determine what it is that we truly want, weigh the cost of obtaining it and then decide whether or not to proceed.

It works like this: first we surround ourselves with a solid social support network, then we learn to think more accurately (hence the cognitive exercise mentioned previously), because then we will have the proper mindset to begin clarifying and blueprinting our life's goals.

The fusion of these three elements creates the *Get Up! College* dynamic so useful in getting unstuck and for beating back (No, more like, *CRUSHING!*) the depressing malaise of mediocrity. In this way we begin building more direction, meaning and power into our lives. It is hard to be bored and depressed when our lives become ordered with a clear sense of dynamic meaning and purpose.

Clearly defined and time bound goals for which you have a passion prompt your brain to powerfully engage. This will help you focus and attract into your life the circumstances and resources necessary to accomplish your objectives.

As Patricia's story (Part Two) so clearly illustrates, it is important to combine action, hard work and lots of inward desire when striving toward your objectives.

Consider transferring, rewriting, printing or photocopying the top ten goals from your journal or organizer onto 3x5 index cards and then tuck them into your purse or wallet. Then review them every day (for a minimum of a year).

You may recall that in a previous chapter we reviewed the importance of duration, frequency, intensity and vividness within the context of imbedding your goals deeply into your mind. Carrying your goals with you permits instant access so that you can review them often, even at a moment's notice.

I maintain my work from the clarifying exercises, together with my goals lists (that is, my Wish List and Blueprint for Life Success) clearly laid out in a binder that I keep in my office at home. I have my top fifteen goals organized on three index cards that I keep in my wallet at all times. Anyone who knows me well can testify to this fact.

Writing down your goals and reviewing them often—in the morning, again at night some time before bed, and during the day whenever you have a few spare moments—impresses them into your mind. This of course activates your internal resources on all levels. Neuroscience informs us that an active brain is a learning brain.

Also, it is *energizing* to review your goals, as it assists with maintaining a positive attitude and a powerful "can do" mindset. The fact of the matter is that if you utilize these techniques, then you won't even have time to be depressed!

Imagine your goals as a reality. See yourself at the goal, enjoying the goal and having achieved the goal. As you do this, you will see positive changes begin to take place and an increased confidence that your goals are indeed achievable.

Even if you stick with a simpler routine (a modification or scaled down version of what we've discussed), you will still be miles ahead of eighty to ninety percent of the population, and well on your way towards a richer, more fulfilling and more enjoyable life.

So as we conclude this chapter, it would be a good time to complete the following:

1. Clarify what it is you want by using the clarifying and mind expanding exercises provided, for example, Magic Pill and Life's Last Days questions.
2. Create your One Page Miracle for the Soul and Wish List.
3. Ask yourself, What Do I Most Enjoy Doing?
4. Identify and list in personal, positive and present tense (using brief sentences) your long-term goals (what you truly want for your life) and the steps (short-term goals)

necessary to get there. Also list the one, two or three things that you first need to accomplish in order to accelerate the accomplishment of your goals (this now becomes your Major Definite Purpose—or MDP).

5. Keep your goals and action steps organized in a binder, journal or notebook so that you can review them daily and make modifications as needed.

6. Create a list of your top five, ten or fifteen goals and place them in your wallet or purse for review in the morning or at night and whenever you get a few spare moments.

7. Develop a daily routine so that you organize your life and attention around your goals.

8. Remember to develop your life blueprint with balance in mind to ensure that you carefully consider all of the important areas of your life, and include these in your life success strategy.

So, "Get Up!" Begin right now to identify what it is that you *truly* want. Create your academic and life success blueprint. Then work on your goals every single day. And always remember the all-important acronym:

Goal

Enriched

Thoughts

Ultimately

Prevail!

CHAPTER FOURTEEN

GET UP! COLLEGE

One of the most important contributions we can make to the profession is to offer effective alternatives to current practice.

-Dr. Patrick McKiernan

As we conclude, by now it ought to be fairly obvious how to best help incoming college freshmen deal with the many challenges, loops, twists and turns that so often accompany college life.

What also ought to be clear is that, unfortunately, few institutions of higher learning employ the kinds of techniques outlined in this audio book in any sort of meaningful way. As a result, millions of students struggle far more than is necessary, resulting in what some researchers can only describe as a national epidemic of increased freshmen college student failure rates.

And to address this issue, we started this audio book by citing research showing that neurological shifts naturally occur in college age youth, often spawning the onset of psychological symptoms, such as anxiety and depression (Jensen, 2015). Such shifts help explain why an otherwise perfectly well-adjusted high school or freshman college student may suddenly experience potentially life-altering psychological symptoms, seemingly out of nowhere.

We also learned from research that students who are the first in their families to attend college often ask themselves, "Do I even belong here?" and "Am I really cut from college cloth?" While other students struggle with loneliness, as well as a whole host of academic and social stressors as they embark upon the college journey.

We've also learned from out time together that out nations' college and university counseling centers are simply too overwhelmed to keep up with growing student mental health needs. And that's why a paradigm shift in the way that mental health services are delivered is now long overdue.

After all, there simply aren't enough college- and university-based mental health professionals to meet student needs as long as traditional one-to-one methods serve as the primary vehicle of intervention. Especially since research, as well as many students and parents that I have interviewed, report that financial stress related to college tuition is becoming an increasingly difficult challenge. And staffing schools with more mental health workers would likely only further escalate college tuition costs.

Instead, the answer lies in helping students develop greater cognitive resilience and the ability to more effectively manage stressors that often serve as a prelude to the development of psychological symptoms. And that's what this book, together with the accompany *Get Up! College* orientation message, boot camps and classes are really all about.

So, instead of expanding student tuition costs, what if college and university administration, counselors, mental health center directors, faculty and support staff received *Get Up! College* program training? In this way, dozens or even hundreds of students could be helped all at one time?

Rapper, Ice Cube, in one of his hit songs, invites the listening audience to, "Check yourself before you wreck yourself!" And so, consistent with Ice Cube's sage advice (as counterintuitive as that may appear to some), this book has sought to "put into check" traditional methods of helping college students navigate the many psychosocial stressors that they are prone to face. This has been done by not only highlighting the problem (that of growing student mental health needs), but also by setting forth student-friendly solutions that research suggests work particularly well.

And again, this is not to say that traditional one-to-one counseling and psychotherapy are obsolete. They aren't. In fact, they are needed now more than ever! But it *is* to say that one-to-one work with students will likely never be enough. The needs of our nations' campuses are simply too voluminous. Therefore, a broader, more positive and student empowering approach is needed.

Get Up! College maximizes the unique formula known as, New Mind Synergy (sometimes referred to as New Life Synergy), created out of Dr. Miller's Southern California private practice. It does so by combining social, cognitive and goals support, three of the most powerful elements indicated by research to work especially well in the lives of students.

It combines them into one program, producing a dynamic and synergistic release of academic and personal potential. The net result to students is greater cognitive resilience and increased personal power (or *dunamis*, a Greek term from which we derive the word, "dynamite").

The word "synergy" also happens to come from an ancient Greek term, *syn-ergos*, which is used to describe the compounding phenomenon of two or more agents (in this case, three agents: social, cognition and goals) that when combined together, achieve considerably more than two or more agents acting independently could achieve, resulting in an end product that is greater than the sum of its parts. Put simply, *Get Up! College* seeks to optimize social, cognitive and goals support in the lives of students in order to help them be more successful.

The *Get Up! College* program for student success is offered in the following ways.

First, to incoming freshmen college students in the form of a dynamic orientation presentation. In this message, students are introduced to important concepts found in *Get Up! College*, and to the school's counseling, health services and various other student support organizations.

Second, *Get Up! College* boot camps are held in communities both large and small. Boot camps are intensive all day events, equipping students with the social, cognitive and goals strategies outlined in this book. In many areas, small group and one-to-one coaching are also offered to students desiring to take the *Get Up! College* strategies to the next level.

Third, the *Get Up! College* class is offered on college and university campuses. It typically takes the form of a training for school personnel, or as a quarter or semester long course for students.

In both on-campus classes and boot camps, students have a chance to experience the most intimate and growth producing interaction available anywhere. Just imagine how a student feel's learning that their struggles are also shared by many of their peers, and that they are not alone. And imagine how students feel upon learning that their greatest struggle can actually become their greatest strength. Students also learn that by practicing simple and easy to use cognitive exercises in the comfort of their own room, they can actually turn a corner on the anxiety and depression that have plagued them for far too long.

And finally, imagine how a student feels when he or she clarifies, by working some of the goals exercises, what they truly want for their life, and what it is that they most want out of their academic experience. Such a transformation is really quite gratifying to witness.

Now students, here's a "quick & clean" snapshot method so that you can begin applying the *Get Up! College* program for success to your life, beginning right now. First, write a list of the most helpful social avenues you can think of—that is, which classes, professors, coaches / mentors, school counselors, friends, family members and groups can you begin to hang out with that will provide a good model for your experience as a student?

Then narrow this list to the top three to five and begin forming these connections immediately. Even though you may become busy, commit to this effort, because in the end, it will pay off *big!*

And if you learn of a *Get Up! College* class being offered at your school or a *Get Up! College* boot camp being offered in your community, then by all means, sign up. I would love to see you there! My organization's website, empowercommunications. org, posts a calendar of *Get Up! College* boot camps and those schools who are hosting the *Get Up! College* class.

Additionally, re-review the chapters on cognition and make a list of the exercises. Then, one by one complete each exercise. Upon completing all of them, identify two or three favorite exercises that you will commit to practicing each and every day. Do this throughout your freshman year and you will absolutely nail it!

In fact, even upon starting this process, you will likely notice an immediate difference in your thoughts. Your mood will lift and you will begin to see things in a more positive and hopeful light.

Also, since happiness is the state of consciousness which proceeds from the achievement of one's values, review the goals exercises as listed above. Work them all. It should take a few days to a few weeks of reflection. Set a timeframe (21 days seems good) by which you will have decided on your primary goals, that is, academic, career, social, financial, lifestyle, etc. and write them down.

Sign your name at the bottom as a commitment and then "burn the bridge" behind you and don't look back! This is a big commitment, so do the exercises with your whole heart and consider these your life's commitment.

Then, write your primary 5, 10 or 15 goals on 3 x 5 index cards and stick them in your binder, journal, wallet or purse. It is imperative that you review these each and every day, morning and night, for the next 1 to 2 years.

And finally, prepare for the dynamic explosion of awakened potential that is sure to be unleashed!

The following story is being shared with you because it represents a culmination of all that we have discussed up to this point.

For Liz Murray, success meant breaking her family cycle of drug addiction, neglect and homelessness.

After years of neglect, wherein Liz and her sister were exposed to their parents' drug abuse and even having to resort to eating such a thing as toothpaste in order to fight off the pangs of hunger, she left home. Liz spent her adolescence in New York sleeping on the streets, in trains and on the couches of friends.

According to Liz, this was a frightening experience, despite the fact that homelessness coursed through her blood by virtue of her family's DNA. As an adolescent her mother had also been homeless and became addicted to drugs at an early age.

Liz recalled that her mother use to often tell her, "One day everything will get better for us. You will see." It was always "One day." But that day never came. In fact, matters would grow worse before getting better.

At the age of sixteen, Liz was served an unnerving wakeup call. In a September 9th 2010 interview aired on NPR's "Talk of the Nation" with host Jennifer Ludden, Liz recounted that after just having buried her mom, she was confronted with the increasingly obvious symmetry of both their lives paths. Liz, as one homeless and set adrift, stated, "I was reliving her life. I was recreating a cycle that I knew had to change. I needed to break this cycle!"

Instead of allowing her painful life circumstances to thrust her further into hopelessness and despair—excusing herself as the product of defective genes, a victim of circumstance who could never possibly amount to anything—she chose to take control of her thoughts and life.

At that moment, Liz made a life transforming decision to get off the streets, return to school and graduate with her high school diploma. In time, and with a lot of hard work and perseverance, she not only graduated from high school, but won a scholarship to Harvard. She graduated from there in 2009. Liz successfully broke the cycle of addiction, neglect and homelessness that had destroyed her family.

Writes legendary football coach Vince Lombardi, "I firmly believe that any man's finest hour—this greatest fulfillment to all he holds dear—is that moment when he has worked his heart out in a good cause and lies exhausted on the field of battle—victorious."

In her memoir, *Breaking Night: A Memoir of Forgiveness, Survival, and My Journey from Homeless to Harvard,* Liz recounts her story in a moving and inspiring way.

Liz is now a motivational speaker and the Founder of Manifest Living, an organization dedicated to inspiring hope and change in people's lives. She points out, "People often believe that their circumstances define who they are, when in reality, that is not the case. . . . People have so much more say so, so much more control over their lives than they often realize." And that is why successfully navigating college all boils down to a choice.

Dear student, regardless of your background—whether you're on shaky ground, like the young Liz Murrays and Chris Millers of the world, or you're an Ivy League hopeful who's well-prepared upon entering college, but wants protection against the potential sudden onslaught of college age psychological symptoms—it is my firm belief that the *Get Up! College* strategies for success will prove invaluable to your endeavors.

These methods worked powerfully for me, and they can work for you too. After all, *If I could it, so can you!*

BIBLIOGRAPHY

ACT. (2012). National collegiate retention and persistence to degree rates. Retrieved January 9, 2014 from http://www.act.org/research/policymakers/pdf/retain_2012.pdf

Amen, D. (2002). *Healing the hardware of the soul.* New York, NY: Free Press.

American College Health Association. (2010). Study of the utilization of student health services. Retrieved April 17, 2014 from http://www.acha.org/topics/docs/acha_benchmarking_report_2010_utilization_survey.pdf

Astin, A.W. (1984). Student involvement: a developmental theory for higher education. *Journal of College Student Personnel, 25,* 297-308.

Astin, A.W. (1993). *What matters in college? four critical years revised.* San Francisco: Jossey Bass.

Bandura, A. (1986). *Social foundations of thought and action: a social cognitive theory.* Upper Saddle River, NJ: Prentice Hall.

Bemish, P.M. (2005). Introduction to the special section—severe and persistent mental illness on college campuses: considerations for service provision. *Journal of College Counseling, 8,* 138-139.

Bean, J.P., & Eaton, S.B. (2001-2002). The psychology underlying successful retention practices. *Journal of College Student Retention, 3,* 73-89.

Beck, A.T., Rush, A. J., Shaw, B.F., & Emery, G. (1979). *Cognitive therapy of depression.* New York: Guilford.

Bohnert, A.M., Aikins, J.W., & Edidin, J. (2007). The role of organized activities in facilitating social adaptation across the transition to college. *Journal of Adolescent Research, 22*, 189-208.

Bonanno, G.A. (2004). Loss, trauma, and human resilience: have we underestimated the human capacity to thrive after extremely aversive events? *American Psychologist, 59*, 20-28.

Boyle, E.T. (2010). Cognitive enhancers. Retrieved November 28, 2010 from www.cogsci.ucsd.edu

Brown, Jennifer L. (2012). Developing a freshman orientation survey to improve student retention within a college. *College Student Journal, 46 (4)*, 834.

Burns, D. (1993). *Ten Days to Self-esteem.* New York, NY: Harper Collins.

Cacioppo, J., Bernston, G., Sheridan, J., & McClintock, M. (2010). Multilevel analysis of human behavior: social neuroscience and the complementing nature of social and biological approaches. *Foundations in Social Neuroscience*, 21-46.

Cadet, D.L. (2008). *Leaving college early or persisting to graduation: A study of African-American men* (Doctoral dissertation). Virginia Commonwealth University.

Campbell, D.J. (1982). Determinates of choice of goal difficulty level: a review of situational and personality influences. *Journal of Occupational Psychology, 55(2)*, 79-95.

Center for the Study of Collegiate Mental Health. (2009). Retrieved November 14, 2010 from http://www.sa.psu.edu/caps/research_center.shtml

Clark, B.R., & Trow, M. (1966). The organizational context. In T.M. Newcomband E.K. Wilson (Eds.), *College peer groups: Problems and prospects for research.* (pp.17-70). Chicago. Aldine Press.

Clore, J.L., & Gaynor, S.T. (2012). Cognitive modification versus therapeutic support for internalizing distress and positive thinking: a randomized technique evaluation trial. *Cognitive Therapy and Research, 36*, 58-71.

Deacon, B.B. (2011). Cognitive defusion versus cognitive restructuring in the treatment of negative self-referential thoughts: an investigation of process and outcome. *Journal of Cognitive Psychotherapy, 25(3)*, 218-232.

DeRubeis, R.J., Hollon, S.D., Amsterdam, J.D., Shelton, R.C., Young, P.R., Salomon, R.M., O'Reardon, J.P., Lovett, M.L., Gladis, M.M., Brown, L.L., & Gallop, R. (2005). Cognitive therapy vs medication in the treatment of moderate to severe depression. *Archives of General Psychiatry, 62(4)*, 409-416.

Diamond, M., & Hopson, J. (1995). *How to Nurture Your Child's Intelligence, Creativity, and Healthy Emotions from Birth Through Adolescence.* New York, NY: Penguin Group.

Dweck, C. S., & Leggett, E. L. (1988). A social-cognitive approach to motivation and personality. *Psychological Review, 95*, 256-273.

Eisenberg, D., Golberstein, E., & Gollust, S.E. (2007). Help-seeking and access to mental health care in a university student population. *Medical Care, 45*, 594-601.

Eisenberg, D., Golberstein, E., & Hunt, J.B. (2009) Mental health and academic success in college. *The B.E. Journal of Economic Analysis & Policy, V. 9, Iss. 1, Contributing Article 40*, 1-35.

Eisenberg, D., Hunt, J., Speer, N., & Zivin, K. (2011). Mental health service utilization among college students in the unites states. *Journal of Nervous and Mental Disease, 199(5)*, 301-308.

Ender, S. C., & Kay, K. (2001). Peer leadership programs: A rationale and review of the literature. In S. L. Hamid (Ed.), *Peer leadership: A primer on program essentials* (Monograph No. 32, pp. 1 – 11). Columbia: University of South, National Resource Center for the First-Year Experience and Students in Transition

Evans, N.J., Forney, D.S., Guido, F.M., & Patton, L.D. (2010). *Student development in college: theory, research, and practice.* San Francisco: Jossey-Bass.

Feldman, K.A., & Newcomb, T.M. (1969). *The impact of college on students.* San Francisco: Jossey-Bass

Freeman, T.M., Anderman, L., & Jensen, J.M. (2007). Sense of belonging in college freshman at the classroom and campus levels. *The Journal of Experimental Education, 75(3),* 203.

Gallagher, R. (2006). National Survey of College Counseling, *The International Association of Counseling Services, Inc. Spring 2006.* Retreived January 22, 2014 from collegecounseling. org/2006-national-survey-of-college-counseling

Gallagher, R. (2010). National Survey of College Counseling, *The International Association of Counseling Services, Inc. Spring 2010.* Retreived March 18, 2014 from www.collegecounseling. org/2010-national-survey-of-college-counseling

Gallagher, R. (2012). National Survey of College Counseling, *The International Association of Counseling Services, Inc. Spring 2012.* Retreived from www. collegecounseling.org/2012-national-survey-of-college-counseling

Goldin, P.R. & Gross, J.J. (2010). *Effects of mindfulness-based stress reduction (mbsr) on emotion regulation in social anxiety disorder. Emotion, 10,* 83-91.

Govindji, R., & Linley, P.A. (2007). Strengths use, self-concordance and well-being: implications for strengths coaching and clinical psychologists. *International Coaching Psychology.*

Gray, D.E., Gabriel, Y., & Goregaokar, H. (2014). Coaching unemployed managers and professionals through the trauma of unemployment: Derailed or undaunted? *Management Learning,* 1-18.

Haglund, M.E.M., Nestadt, P.S., Cooper, N.S., Southwick, S.M., & Charney, D.S. (2007). Psychobiological mechanisms of resilience: relevance to prevention and treatment of stress-related psychopathology. *Development and Psychopathology, 19*, 3.

Hannum, J.W., & Dvorak, D.M. (2004). Effects of family conflict, divorce, and attachment patterns on the psychological distress and social adjustment of college freshman. *Journal of College Student Development, 45*, 27-42.

Hartley, M.T. (2011). Examining the relationships between resilience, mental health, and academic persistence in undergraduate college students. *Journal of American College Health, 59*, 596-604.

Hartley, M.T. (2012). Assessing and promoting resilience: an additional tool to address the increasing number of college students with psychological problems. *Journal of College Counseling, 15(1)*, 37-51.

Hintz, J. R. (2011). Peer educators responding to an institutional challenge: Off-campus student services. *New Directions for Student Services*, 133, 87-95. doi: 10.1002/ss.387

Hirsch, K., & Barton, A. (2011). Positive social support, negative social exchanges, and suicidal behavior in college students. *Journal of American College Health, 58(5)*, 393-398.

Hollon, S.D., Stewart, M.O., & Strunk, D. (2006). Enduring effects for cognitive behavior therapy in the treatment of depression and anxiety. *Annual Review of Psychology, 57*, 285-315.

Hollon, S.D., Thase, M.E., & Markowitz, J.C. (2002). Treatment and prevention of depression. *Psychological Science in the Public Interest, 3(2)*, 39-77.

Howard, K.I., Kopta, S.M., Krause, M.S., & Orlinsky, D.E. (1986). The dose effect relationship in psychology. *American Psychologist, 41(2)*, 159-164.

Horowitz, J.L., & Garber, J. (2006). The prevention of depressive symptoms in children and adolescents: a meta-analytic review. *Journal of Consulting and Clinical Psychology, 74(3)*, 401-415.

Hughes, J., Gourley, M., Madson, L., & Le Blanc, K. (2011). Stress and coping activity: reframing negative thoughts. *Society for the Teaching of Psychology*, *38(1)*, 36-39.

Hunt, M.G., Ertel, E., Coello, J.A., & Rodriguez, L. (2014). Empirical support for a self-help treatment for IBS. *Cognitive Therapy and Research*, October 19, 2014 Issue.

Jenkins, D., Zeidenberg, M., & Wachen, J. (2009). *Educational outcomes of Cabrillo College's Digital Bridge Academy: Findings from a multivariet analysis.* New York, NY: Community College Research Center, Teacher's College, Columbia University.

Jensen, E. (2005). *Teaching with the brain in mind.* Alexandria, VA: ASCD.

Jensen, F. (2015). *The teenage brain.* New York, NY: HarperCollins Publishers.

Karakowsky, L., & Mann, S.L. (2008). Setting goals and taking ownership: understanding the implications of participatively setting goals from a causal attribution perspective. *Journal of Leadership & Organizational Studies*, *14*, 260-270.

Kraft, D. P. (2009). Mens Sana: the growth of mental health in the american college health association. *Journal of American College Health*, *58*(3), 267-275.

Laible, D.J., Carlo, G., & Raffaelli, M. (2009). The differential relations of parent and peer attachment to adolescent adjustment. *Journal of Youth & Adolescence. 29*, 45-59.

Latham, G.P., & Locke, E.A. (2007). New developments in and directions for goal-setting research. *European Psychologist, 12*, 290-300.

Leaf, C. (2009). *The gift in you.* Southlake, TX: Improv, LTD.

Leaf Interview with Ali Brown (2010). *Clean out your brain! Control your toxic thoughts and emotions for best success.*

Lidy, K.M., & Kahn, J.H. (2006). Personality as a predictor of first-semester adjustment to college: the meditational role of perceived social support. *Journal of College Counseling, 9,* 123-124.

Lightsey, O.R., Jr. (1997). Stress buffers and dysphoria: A prospective study. *The Journal of Cognitive Psychotherapy, 11,* 263-277.

Linley, P.A. (2008). Positive changes following adversity. *PTSD Research Quarterly, 21(3),* 1-3.

Linley, P. A., Nielsen, K. M., Wood, A. M., Gillett, R., & Biswas-Diener, R. (2010). Using signature strengths in pursuit of goals: effects on goal progress, need satisfaction, and wellbeing, and implications for coaching psychologists. *International Coaching Psychology Review, 5*(1), 8-17.

Locke, E.A., & Latham, G.P. (1990, 2002). New directions in goal-setting theory. *Current Directions in Psychological Science, 15,* 5.

Masten, A.S. (2001). Ordinary magic: resilience processes in development. *American Psychologist, 56,* 227-238.

Mattanah, J.F., Ayers, J.F., Brand, B.L., Brooks, L.J., Quimby, J.L., McNary, S. (2010). A social support intervention to ease the college transition: exploring main effects and moderators. *Journal of College Student Development, 52,* 93-108.

Miller, C. (2011). *I've fallen and I can get up! the ultimate life recovery program.* Bloomington, Indiana: WestBow Press.

Miller, C. (2014). *Vote Captain US 2.0.* Los Angeles, CA: Empower Communications Network (ECN).

Morin, A. (2005). Possible links between self-awareness and inner speech: theoretical background, underlying mechanisms, and empirical evidence. *Journal of Consciousness Studies, 12,* 115-134.

Morisano, D., Hirsch, B., Peterson, J., Pihl, R., & Shore, M. (2010). Setting, elaborating, and reflecting on personal goals improves academic performance. *Journal of Applied Psychology*, *95(2)*, 255-264.

Myers, S. B., Sweeney, A. C., Popick, V., Wesley, K., Borfeld, A., & Fingerhut, R. (2012). Self-care practices and perceived stress levels among psychology graduate students. *Training and Education in Professional Psychology*, *6(1)*, 55-66.

National Center for Public Policy and Higher Education. (2012). Retrieved May 9, 2014 from www.highereducation.org

Navarro, D. (2012). Supporting the students of the future. Retrieved February 13, 2014 from www.changemag.org

Nicholls, J.G. (1984). Achievement motivation: conceptions of ability, subjective experience, task choice, and performance. *Psychological Review*, *91*, 328-346.

NPR Interview with Liz Murray. Aired September 9, 2010.

Pascarella, E.T., & Terenzini, P.T. (1991). *How college affects students.* Jossey-Bass: San Francisco.

Peele, S. (1992). Alcoholism, politics, and bureaucracy: The consensus against controlled-drinking therapy in America. *Addictive Behaviors*, *17*, 49-62.

Perry, R. P. (1991). Perceived control in college students: Implications for instruction in higher education. In J. Smart (Ed.), *Higher education: Handbook of theory and research.* New York: Agathon Press.

Reik, W., Dean, W., & Walter, J. (2001). Epigenetic reprogramming in mammalian development. *Science*, *293*, 1089-1093.

Schneider, R. (2010). *Usefulness of high school average and ACT scores in making college admissions decisions.* ACT Research Report Series, 2010-2.

Seaward, B.L. (2006). *Stress Management: Principles and strategies for health and well-being* (5th ed.). Boston, MA: Jones & Bartlett.

Seligman, M.E.P., Ernst, R.M., Gillham, J., Reivich, K., & Linkins, M. (2009). Positive education: positive psychology and classroom interventions. *Oxford Review of Education, 35(3),* 293-311.

Shook, J.L., Keup, J.R. (2012). The benefits of peer leader programs: an overview from the literature. *Peer Leadership in higher Education, 2012(157),* 5-16.

Shyh Shin, W. (2010). Balanced states of mind in psychopathology and psychological well-being. *Journal of Psychology, 45(4),* 269-277.

Snyder, C.R., & Lopez, S.J. (2007). *Positive psychology: the scientific and practical exploration of human strengths.* Thousand Oaks, CA, US: Sage Publications.

Strunk, D.R., Brotman, M.A., DeRubeis, R.J., & Hollon, S.D. (2010). Therapist competence in cognitive therapy for depression: Predicting subsequent symptom change. *Journal of Consulting and Clinical Psychology, 78,* 429-437

Stupnisky, R.H., Renaud, R.D., Perry, R.P., Ruthig, J.C., Haynes, T.L., & Clifton, R.A. (2007). Comparing self-esteem and perceived control as predictors of first-year college students' academic achievement. *Social Psychology of Education, 10(3),* 303-330.

Suomi, S. (1999). Attachment in rhesus monkeys. In J. Cassidy & P. Shaver (Eds.), *Handbook of Attachment.* New York, NY: Guilford Press.

Tinto, V. (1975). Dropout from higher education: a theoretical synthesis of recent research. *Review of Educational Research, 75,* 89-125.

Tinto, V. (2001). *Rethinking the first year of college.* Higher Education Monograph Series: Syracuse University.

Tinto, V. (2006-2007). Research and practice of student retention: what next? *Journal of College Student Retention, 8(1),* 1-19.

Tolin, D.F. (2010). Is cognitive-behavioral therapy more effective than other therapies?: a meta-analytic review. *Clinical Psychology Review, 30(6)*, 710-720.

Tonson & Taylor (2007). Molecular mechanisms of memory consolidation. *Nature Reviews Neuroscience*, 8, 262-275.

Tracy, B. (2003). *The Ultimate Goals Program*. Niles, IL: Nightingale-Conant.

Whiteman, S.D., Barry, A.E., Mroczek, D.K., & MacDermid Wadsworth, S. (2013). The development and implications of peer emotional support for student service members/veterans and civilian college students. *Journal of Counseling Psychology, 60*, 265-278.

Witthoft, M., Basfeld, C., Steinhoff, M., & Gerlach, A. (2012). Can't suppress this feeling: automatic negative evaluations of somatosensory stimuli are related to the experience of somatic symptom distress. *Emotion, 12(3)*, 640-649.

Wong, S.S. (2010). Balanced states of mind in psychopathology and psychological well-being. *International Journal of Psychology, 45(4)*, 269-277.

Woosley, S.A. (2003). How important are the first few weeks of college? The long term effects of initial college experiences. *College Student Journal, 37(2)*, 201-207.

VISIT DR. CHRIS ONLINE

WWW.ECNCOUNSELING.COM

- EDUCATIONAL CONSULTING
- CULTURAL IMPACT
- DYNAMIC SPEAKING